RATTLE

Poetry for the 21st Century

Issue #32

Volume 15, Number 2

Winter 2009

EDITOR-IN-CHIEF
Alan Fox

EDITOR
Timothy Green

ASSISTANT EDITOR
Megan O'Reilly Green

EDITOR EMERITUS
Stellasue Lee

ARTWORK
Stacie Primeaux

EDITORIAL ASSISTANT
Cassandra Glickman

PROOFING ASSISTANCE
Jeffrey Gerretse
Karen Green
Jacquelyn Lazo

DISTRIBUTORS:

Armadillo & Co. Distrib
(310) 693-6061
7310 S. La Cienega Blvd
Inglewood, CA 90302

Ingram Periodicals
(800) 627-6247
18 Ingram Blvd
La Vergne, TN 37090

Ubiquity Distributors
(718) 875-5491
607 Debgraw St.
Brooklyn, NY 11217

Winter, 2009, Vol. 15, No. 2

All rights revert to authors on publication. *RATTLE* features poetry, translations, reviews, essays and interviews. Send submissions and orders to *RATTLE*, 12411 Ventura Blvd., Studio City, CA 91604. All work must be accompanied by a SASE, cover letter and bio, and is welcome all year. Payment for work accepted is two contributor copies. *RATTLE* accepts simultaneous submissions, and email submissions, but all work must be previously unpublished. For more information visit:

www.*RATTLE*.com

Printed in Canada by
Printcrafters/Westcan Printing Group
78 Hutchings Street
Winnipeg, Manitoba R2X 3B1
Canada
(866) 337-1170

RATTLE

Poetry for the 21st Century

TABLE OF CONTENTS

POETRY

Cristin O'Keefe Aptowicz	*At the Office Holiday Party*	9
Michael Bazzett	*The Disintegrated Man*	10
Francesca Bell	*With a Little Education*	11
Tammy F. Brewer	*One of Those Topics I Shouldn't Talk About*	12
Erik Campbell	*This Small Thing*	14
Claire W. Donzelli	*Two Haiku*	17
Christine Dresch	*Nuts*	18
Laura Eve Engel	*Did You Come Yet?*	20
Joseph Fasano	*North Country*	21
Matthew Gavin Frank	*After Senza Titolo, 1964*	23
Glenn J. Freeman	*The Transparencies*	25
Ed Galing	*Dancing*	26
Peter Harris	*Living Large*	28
Lilah Hegnauer	*Exceptions with the Sloughing Off*	29
Michael Hettich	*The Wild Animal*	30
Bob Hicok	*How the Mirror Looks This Morning*	31
Colette Inez	*The Tuner*	32
John Philip Johnson	*Midas on the Beach*	33
Michael Kriesel	*Threesome*	35
Rachel Inez Lane	*Catch Me, Alfred, I'm Falling*	36
Ken Letko	*The Power of Light*	38
M	*Salt*	39
Marie-Elizabeth Mali	*Campaign Season*	41
Kerrin McCadden	*Intersection*	42
Laren McClung	*Confluence of Rivers and Mouths*	43
Sally Molini	*Meal Ticket*	44
Kent Newkirk	*Fixing Cars*	45
Molly Peacock	*A Tale of a T*	46
	The Softie	47
J. F. Quackenbush	*To a Child*	49
Rebekah Remington	*Happiness Severity Index*	51
David Romtvedt	*On Broadway*	52
Ralph James Savarese	*Nor Yet a Dream of War*	53
Lauren Schmidt	*Grandma Zolie Gives Unheeded Advice*	58
Mather Schneider	*Between Us and It*	59
Prartho Sereno	*Electrodomestico*	60
Lee Sharkey	*Berlioz*	62
Paul Siegell	*06.25.00 – PHiSH – Alltel Pavilion, NC*	63
Charlie Smith	*The Casing*	64
John L. Stanizzi	*S-Plan*	65
Arthur Vogelsang	*Environmental*	69
David Wagoner	*Before the Poetry Reading*	70
Mike White	*Nascar*	71
Jeff Worley	*Lucky Talk*	72

RATTLE POETRY PRIZE WINNER

Lynne Knight	*To the Young Man Who Cried Out...*	75

HONORABLE MENTIONS

Michelle Bitting	*Mammary*	79
Mary-Lou Brockett-Devine	*Crabs*	81
Carolyn Creedon	*How to Be a Cowgirl in a Studio Apartment*	83
Douglas Goetsch	*Writer in Residence, Central State*	85
David Hernandez	*Remember It Wrong*	87
John Paul O'Connor	*Beans*	89
Howard Price	*Crow-Magnon*	90
Patricia Smith	*Birthday*	91
Alison Townsend	*The Only Surviving Recording...*	92
Emily Kagan Trenchard	*This Is the Part of the Story...*	94

TRIBUTE TO THE SONNET

T. S. Davis	*The Recrudescence of the Muse*	97
Tony Barnstone	*Bad Usage*	107
Michelle Bitting	*Silence Took My Tongue...*	109
Chris Bullard	*Back Story*	110
Wendy Taylor Carlisle	*The Circus of Inconsolable Loss*	111
Peter Coghill	*Gabriella*	112
T. S. Davis	*Whooping Rendezvous*	113
Paul Dickey	*A Knack for Losing Things*	114
Caitlin Doyle	*Backward Sonnet for a Forward Thinker*	115
Jehanne Dubrow	*The Cold War, A Romance*	116
Alan Fox	*Dover*	117
Carol Frith	*Black Tights, a Halter Top*	118
Ernest Hilbert	*Cover to Cover*	119
Luke Johnson	*The Heart, Like a Bocce Ball*	120
Mollycat Jones	*Unholy Sonnet Number One*	121
Stephen Kessler	*Any Hack Can Crank Out a Hundred Sonnets*	122
Jeff Knight	*Knives of the Poets*	123
Gregory Loselle	*from The Whole of Him Collected*	124
Austin MacRae	*Library Lovers*	125
Patti McCarty	*Make Mine Darjeeling*	126
Mary Meriam	*The Romance of Middle Age*	127
Jessica Moll	*Costume*	128
Ron Offen	*Aubade for One Dismayed*	129
Jessica Piazza	*Panophilia*	130
Catherine Esposito Prescott	*To a Hurricane*	131
Patricia Smith	*Motown Crown*	132
Elizabeth Klise von Zerneck	*Freedom*	140
Thom Ward	*Rumpus, Cohesion, Mess*	141
Donald Mace Williams	*The Venturi Effect*	142
John Yohe	*The Ghost of Frank O'Hara*	143

CONVERSATIONS WITH ALAN FOX

Alice Fulton	147
Molly Peacock	165

Contributor Notes	181

POETRY

Cristin O'Keefe Aptowicz

AT THE OFFICE HOLIDAY PARTY

I can now confirm that I am not just fatter
than everyone I work with, but I'm also fatter
than all their spouses. Even the heavily bearded
bear in accounting has a lithe otter-like boyfriend.

When my co-workers brightly introduce me
as "the funny one in the office," their spouses
give them a look which translates to, *Well, duh*,
then they both wait for me to say something funny.

A gaggle of models comes shrieking into the bar
to further punctuate why I sometimes hate living
in this city. They glitter, a shiny gang of scissors.
I don't know how to look like I'm not struggling.

Sometimes on the subway back to Queens,
I can tell who's staying on past the Lexington stop
because I have bought their shoes before at Payless.
They are shoes that fool absolutely no one.

Everyone wore their special holiday party outfits.
It wasn't until I arrived at the bar that I realized
my special holiday party outfit was exactly the same
as the outfits worn by the restaurant's busboys.

While I'm standing in line for the bathroom,
another patron asks if I'm there to clean it.

Michael Bazzett

THE DISINTEGRATED MAN

for Marvin Bell

The disintegrated man was, at one time, integrated.
He was as solid as a river stone, as the white pages of a manuscript
　　　stacked like a brick on the table.
　　　His edges were crisp.
Now the disintegrated man crumbles like softened wood,
　　　like the toppled oak melting into loam.
His trunk seethes with the shining backs of beetles, burrowing.
No, there is nothing staccato about the disintegrated man.

In his dream, black hominids scuttle over mountains in a landfill.
They move along invisible trails, like endless trains of ants.
The black hominids move with the monotonous momentum
　　　of unpunctuated sentences.
　　　Their dark lines seem to sizzle.
Though the disintegrated man dreams, he does not sleep. He is vigilant,
　　　and numb.
The banjo strum of his heart is not plucked.
Even poignant melodies bounce off his lungs, unable to seize them
　　　with yearning.

His identical cousin, the dead man, is more blasé. He floats
　　　in the chamber of memory, iridescent
　　　as veils of oil spread on a pond.
The disintegrated man does not float. He is corporeal
　　　and becomes the hibiscus, the stamen, the waxy egg of the butterfly.

The dead man dwells within a synapse. He flickers
across the white screen of the synapse, but does not change.
The disintegrated man wonders why, once at rest,
　　　Jesus bothered to come back.

The dead man does not wonder, but reflects.
Sometimes he is young, and sprints like a dog across the open fields.
He does not crumple, or snag his toe on a root.

The disintegrated man has no time for such shenanigans.
He is feeding the horde of thousands that depend upon him.
He feeds the grub, and the meaty root, and returns, in increments, to the
　　　world.

Francesca Bell

WITH A LITTLE EDUCATION

This is what became of that homely high school boy
with the fine hands and big brain. He ended up sliding
his fingers all day into the vaginas of other men's wives.
Expensive women who book six months in advance
to take off their clothes for him. He keeps them
waiting under a harsh light and thin sheet
before delivering their silver-spoon babies and bad news,
before roving his skilled hands over all that cheerful flesh
that used to be firmly out of his reach. They send him
flowers now and page him after hours, tell him
when their sex lives are painful or dry up entirely.
He coaches them to remind their deal-making,
deposition-taking husbands of the grave
importance of foreplay. He touches their sleeves
as they leave with what could only be mistaken
for tenderness, and smiles, knowing they wonder
what he does with his hands at night. How different
his landscape looks now: his rolling stool like a throne,
the world he has mastered spread glorious before him.
If only he had known, back when he was pimpled
and pained that even the hearts of the beautiful burn
in the third trimester, and that age bursts
in without mercy on everyone, even those girls
as effervescent and confusing as champagne.
If only he could have imagined how easy
it would be, with a little education,
to wake each morning to a string of women
naked in his office and ready just for him.

Tammy F. Brewer

ONE OF THOSE TOPICS I SHOULDN'T TALK ABOUT

To be honest, there are times when
I say to myself God I hope I'm not

pregnant. My faith is not 100%
in condoms. Why I never had sex

until I was 19. And then I married him
several years later. We have a son now

and I remember when I told him the news.
I came out of the bathroom saying, "Look

what you did!" Pointing the plastic wand
as though he was the only one

responsible. That's the word that comes
to mind after I hope I'm not pregnant.

Even at 33 I think I should know better
except the pill really screws up my body.

So I choose not to take it. For a long time
I didn't know what it was to ovulate. Now

my body is like clockwork. Always
two weeks after my period and I tell him

we have to be careful. Responsibilities.
In high school health class we learned

how to give life by blowing air into a dummy's
mouth. That same year they erected

a Coke machine in the school cafeteria.
Because everyone likes to have Coke.

"But not sex!" my dad said after he found
Ann's birth control pills in her room. "No

daughter of mine is having it!" To be invisible
is to not be pregnant. Because when you are

pregnant, strangers touch your belly and tell you
what you should and should not do

when the baby comes. Before I know I'm not
pregnant I imagine how my life might be

different. Like changing lanes all of a sudden
when another car doesn't see me.

When you have a child you worry about space
in the backseat and whether there is too much

sunlight or not enough. I pull the seatbelt tight
across my chest, look at my son in the rearview mirror:

An American flag sways its head back-and-forth
in front of the Georgia Right To Life headquarters. Next door

a young Hispanic girl looks through the window of a T.V.
repair shop, hair parted unevenly down the middle. Her father

waits in the gravel parking lot, car idling. The trunk
open and empty.

Erik Campbell

THIS SMALL THING
for my father (1942-2007)

I. *This Small Thing*

It was strange to me that the nurses
could shave him but weren't allowed to

trim his nails. He was so thin by this time
he resembled his always thinner twin brother,

who, fighting the future, never visited.
Everything about him was now small,

save for his nails. His face free of
its hieroglyphics and ruddiness, all

stories and sadness bleached, smooth
as watered stone. I sat there for four hours

holding his hand, his fingernails digging
into my palm, hurting me. But he didn't

know, and hadn't known anything for days.
He squeezed my hand, maybe thinking

of his mother and when her hand meant
warmth and unnamable things. I couldn't

know. But I remember fearing then that
the sum of us is mechanistic. That dust

makes eyes water as easily as death. I was
so eager to inhabit his hand grasping

mine with meaning, to anthropomorphize
my own father, which sounds ridiculous,

but might be what we must do. When
morphine finally loosened his grip,

I clipped his fingernails. His toenails next.
One thought only as I worked: God

damn it. And God damn it. You will not
claw your way out of this world.

II. *Rooms*

There will be a life
you did not choose;

it will include
many rooms.

There will be a room
you will not leave;

it will be a room
you did not choose.

III. *After*

Don't regret what you did
not find, say, a secret
diary where he
unpacked his thoughts
in the private, melodic
voice you always wanted,
something that might
resolve his silences,
pathologize his sighs.
By now I've searched
the whole house
and found only lint.
But I can tell you this:

when you're later given
one of his jackets,
check the pockets first
thing. You might find

a match or a Jolly Rancher.
You might find more lint.
It doesn't matter
what you find, only

that you found it
and know it isn't
a gift or a clue.

Claire W. Donzelli

TWO HAIKU

Birdhouse

Round worn wooden frame
Spirals up to a cone roof.
Dark vacant window.

Gas Leak

Gas leak in the air
Water chilled as a river
Grace is unaware

Christine Dresch

NUTS

The last few months, my grandfather
answered only to the name
General Anthony Clement McAuliffe,
101st Airborne Division commander
during the Battle of the Bulge.
Nazis were endlessly besieging the nursing home.
He haunted the front lobby,
ducking the muzzle flash of passing chrome,
rallying brigades to repel visiting doctors,
telling the nurses they could stick
their Kraut applesauce up their Kraut asses.

General McAuliffe was real enough,
and widely remembered for replying "Nuts!"
to German demands for surrender.
So we guessed he might have
met the general, over there.
Maybe he'd fought in Belgium—
the massacre at Malmedy, the Wereth 11—
an awful lot had been going on.
We questioned old friends,
but we never found out for sure.
He rarely mentioned the war;
all he'd ever kept he black-bagged
in the attic, immaculately pressed,
looking hardly worn.

I suppose it's never too early
to begin talking myself into
whatever person will confront
what I'll no longer be capable of fending off.
Sometimes I lean towards Oprah,
reinforced by whooping housewives,
or Annie Oakley,
blowing holes in buffalo nickels.
Other times I think
I'd like to be Mae West,
embarrassing the attendants
rolling me to BINGO
with suggestive jests.

But on days when distant
seems to have crept a bit closer
since last I looked, I think it might
be wisest to end up Amelia Earhart
who, long after her final takeoff,
could still be glimpsed via a fiery, jeweled trail
arcing the vanishing point of sea and sky,
leaving no wreckage behind.

Laura Eve Engel

DID YOU COME YET?

I should have brought a book to read instead
of counting ceiling tiles, half-undressed.
The sooner through, the sooner we're to bed.

I swear I yawned until my face was red,
then coughed a bit, but you were not impressed.
I should have brought a book. To read. Instead,

I strategically placed my migraine meds
in plain view. Ok, on my breasts.
The sooner through, the sooner we're to bed.

If you had read me better than you did,
you'd know the thing I want's not you, but rest.
I should have brought a book. To read (instead)

the sounds you made just inches from my head
used to drive me wild. Now it's a test.
The sooner through, the sooner we're to bed.

It frightens me that what we have's half-dead.
We cut the foreplay, why not cut the rest?
I should have brought a book to read. Instead,
I wrote this poem. Come, love. To bed.

Joseph Fasano

NORTH COUNTRY

Tonight the moon smells like the forehead
of an idiot savant
they dragged from a car wreck last week
on the road to Monticello.

No wind. No flock.
But buck-blind slug-crack.

The house they're leveling by the power plant:
a woman who starved herself

kept her father there
four winters, his trashed lung
filling her sleep with a blue whir.

Once, after his burial, I saw her in the yard
crouched over the frozen carcass of a groundhog

that had opened its gut
on the deer fence, stumbled a few yards,

and sprawled out, bewildered,
by the garbage lid.

I couldn't hear what she was saying,
and still can't,
but when she rose to turn back I watched her
bend down again

and crush her cigarette into the bushy scarab
of a face, slowly, twice in each eye.

It was February. Bucks
hung from an oak.

And because I think there's no harm
in misunderstanding,
I think maybe that's what poverty
meant to her:

the body's going back. The scar
and the rush.

The going back so quietly the hour
will never know how innocent
you think you are.

Matthew Gavin Frank

AFTER SENZA TITOLO, 1964

painting by Corrado Cagli

I promised him I would not say
grasshopper, or superman. So

Fortune is this fish and this
flower, and neither are the body—

not some smart flat
of a knife. Not some

wondering about the stars.
The coming into the world

insectile, or some dumb gang
of coral, smacked with its first air—

I can't look at a fish without thinking
how lucky they are to have

the ocean. How can they watch
the stars? It's beautiful

what must be substitute,
their words for night,

the different way they
hold their fins.

How we come into
this thin tissue with a stroke

of fingertip over gill, the words
we have to explain, dumb

as the coral—wing to bird, fin
to fish, leaf to tree—is that

the best we can do?
Our heartbreak is last year's

nest, the frozen lake, the yard
we forgot to rake. The lie

is that we'll miss our families most.
Instead: the silver batteries

agitating the surface of the water,
the things we aren't—some wild

mating we can only read about,
all strange biology and our hearts

that are a part of it, kept from us,
something else we're not. We're

made up of servants
without a lord, working to push us

toward cold water and
it's beautiful, we're science

and there is no substitute
for the stars. Not mother

or husband or daughter, but fish,
but finch, but fir.

Glenn J. Freeman

THE TRANSPARENCIES

In the Encyclopedia Britannica I used as a kid,
the body was built in layers of transparency,
a skeletal foundation you could overlap
with, one by one, the circulatory system,
the muscles, the organs, the flesh—
or, likewise, you could peel away from the whole
and leave only bone, two full spreads, of course,
one for each sex. Hours I spent
with the glossy images, lifting up or laying down
as if there in the shiny representations of bone & flesh
I might find where it starts.
A simple Google search for anatomy or human
body and a million images now appear, labels
and diagrams and 3-D graphics and moving parts—
and then there's the plastinated bodies, corpses
frozen in their simple routines without flesh,
muscles and veins engaging with the everyday.
Sure, it's easy to proclaim the miracle of the human
body, or even the faith or belief
that emerges from somewhere deep within it,
but something different altogether to imagine
the layers of history folded like those transparencies
into each self—but that's too forceful
a metaphor I didn't even intend, one I didn't own
even as I set out to remember
what haunted me as a child, that fragment
of a memory now a keepsake, a phantom
somewhere beyond the peeling away, some empty
space beneath the final page, beneath the hollow
of bones where I'd gladly return for one touch
of that initial mystery, even if it meant pulling away
that sheet so that nothing remained, all gone down
like history into the dust and loam.

Ed Galing

DANCING

it was a marathon,
and we did it right off
Broadway in New York, back
when apples were sold on
street corners by haggard
looking men who never shaved
anymore, standing on street
corners, the lines were long
back then, waitin for a free
turkey from the salvation army
for thanksgiving,
      people were
flyin upside down from airplanes,
and there was a guy called Shipwreck
Kelley sittin on a flagpole, way
up, for weeks, rain or shine,
just to see how long he could
stay up there, hopin to make a
buck that way,
      my girl and I got into the
dance marathon...
      picture a rickety hall, with
fifty young people like us,
dancing day and night, holdin on to
each other till we dropped, hell,
this went on day and night, and
the winner would get a few hundred
bucks, while the sister promoters
made the most of it, and the
loud music comin from a jukebox,
day and night, around and around we
went, and pathe news showed us on
the screen, and walter winchell
wrote us up, and nobody really
gave a shit about any of this,
seeing how everybody was crazy in
them days anyway,
      on the fifth day of dancing
most of the contestants had dropped
out, the meat wagon took em away,
imagin women hangin on to their
boyfriends, around the neck, while

the boyfriend dragged his partner
around and around like a bunch of
damn zombies.

there was a fifteen minute break
so we could do what we had to do,
goin around the room, foxtrot,
waltz, mostly, and we all had
these big damn numbers on our
backs,

near the end, before my girl
and I dropped out, my feet were
swollen the size of an elephant's,
and my partner looked like she
was gonna faint any minute,

like she was gonna die right
then and there, hell, i was draggin
her around like a dust mop,

at the end of this dance
marathon the cops finally came
around and closed the whole damn
thing up...the mayor said it was
inhuman for people to dance like
this, just to see who could last
longer,

we got nuthin for our dancing
and it wasn't very pretty,

we broke up after that,
and I joined the navy, figurin
let the government take care of
me, and I would look good in a
sailor suit,

and last I heard, my partner
was workin in a night club somewhere,
tryin to make out as a singer

and the place where we danced
was sold at an auction and it's bare
and quiet now there, and the world
keeps on goin around and around.

and this is where I get off.

Peter Harris

LIVING LARGE

The father's princess was ready to quit
his palace with only a ribbed pullover,
drawstring pants, three-quarters
of a degree, and a Peruvian shawl,

leaving behind his blundering ballet
of lasso love, also her hoop earrings,
her made-up mom, and 20 eloquent
pairs of trainers, pumps and clogs,

leaving behind the mahogany niche
in his law firm, off to become Tibetan,
ready to practice opening her throat
wide enough to chant three notes at once.

What's wrong with this? He gestured
to his courtyard with its cherub fountain.
"Dad, if you could ride the back of a whale,
would you shimmy life away
like the koi fish your cherub's always peeing on?"

Dad's gill slits began to slam open
and shut in the foyer of his chateau
in Grosse Point Shores. He shouted,
"Is that what I am to you, just some
goldfish? Is that what I am?"

But she'd already hopped into her cab
whose tires spat tiny showers
of white pebbles back at him.
The courtyard would have to be raked again.

Lilah Hegnauer

EXCEPTIONS WITH THE SLOUGHING OFF

Never before had we been so angular and ready and situated,
never in the same way watching and watching
under the eaves wrapped in aluminum, paper flowers,
your ease with the *Times*. For thirty minutes: no more,

I took your corner tightly and felt like a criminal
undone with the scattering of seed. Looking back
I should never have stayed. Once round again, once more
it seemed to me that stay and go were the best

options: both of them. It seemed we were waiting
on some misdirected train to sweep over the hearth
and add its cookies to our picnic basket and say *now
now now*. Or we were waiting for a sleepyhead. Or we

were waiting for everybody to finish their lemonade
and head out. We waited and waited. We asked nothing
of the time except that it let us make down the bed
each night and steal our neighbor's blackberries

and if we were a little droopy in the drawers it was
only because we lacked relevance. Our lives seemed
to exist next to our lives. Our lives rented
the guest cottage in our lives' backyard, three terraces

down in the lowest garden. To explain: in another year
or era, I might have fished gumballs out of my pockets
and tossed them to endless children who popped out
from behind every imaginable crevice. I did.

Michael Hettich

THE WILD ANIMAL

They knock over everything, boys and girls,
hardly more than instruments waiting to be played;
hardly more than rivers waiting to be navigated,
waiting to be damned; hardly more than songs
waiting for their harmony; hardly more than eyes.
I lived inside the hope of rain, she says. I lived inside
the gesture of a fisherman casting out his line.
The bait was still alive and swam frantically and bled
as the tide reached its arms out and gathered up the seaweed
filled with tiny creatures and stories of the depth of things
where you and the other world, the one without end
without end became mesmerized, covered in a pelt of fur
no one had a name for. So they called you Wild Animal
and wondered what you'd do now, how you'd manage to survive,
and they watched you carefully, and they gave you fancy names
in an otherwise forgotten language, as they tracked your *slow demise*
otherwise known as extinction.

Bob Hicok

HOW THE MIRROR LOOKS THIS MORNING

Probably the size of the six volt
made it seem life-giving. I had wires, a drawer
of red and green and black wires
in a thicket where socks belonged,
I had this idea that a six volt battery
would bring the cat back to life
and cut it down from where it hung

but nothing, even when I put wires
in anus and mouth, even when I touched
the Xs of its eyes
with copper. I can ask now
why I believed that,
or why I killed the cat
in the first place, or why can't I travel
at the speed of sound? The kitty
that comes around every evening for food
purrs closer and closer
to my rehabilitation. God, on the other hand,

sent a train into a bus last night,
if you believe in God, in trains, in time
as something that can be broken down
into units, and spoken of, and held
as much as anything can be held,
can anything be held
that doesn't cut through what asks
to hold it? Twenty-two dead,
and yet I think of myself
as a happy person.

Colette Inez

THE TUNER
for E.C.

Choose how the forest
was deprived of a tree.
Blight, wind, fire?
I once lost a cantankerous man,
who tuned pianos.
Tall, an oak to me,
he goaded music from the keys.
I almost see him biting on his pipe,
tamping down the London Dock.
Blown back leaves, birds, moths,
the gestures here.
Pendulum, tool box auctioned off.
Summer roars another blast of green.
"I like to see a piano perspire,"
he'd say to me, slamming the lid
of the Baldwin.

John Philip Johnson

MIDAS ON THE BEACH

When Midas went to the beach
everyone in his kingdom was nervous.
They liked the foot-shaped patches of golden sand,
scooped up like cattle patties,
and they were used to the nimble ruckus
of the entourage, staying somewhat close
but avoiding the bump. Their fear was for the sea,
for his first step, for the yellow muck hardening
around his ankles like it did in his brief Saturday night baths.
They would rescue him, of course, if the water trapped his feet—
throw him chains which they would later add to the treasury
once he'd grabbed them and been dragged
over the sharp, concreted waves.
It was a matter of some speculation for them,
but as he stared across the water,
their anxiety rose, and they muttered
about the loss of the fishing industry,
imagining the blue sea becoming gold.

It was the philosopher's punishment, anyway:
He'd been estranged with his daughter
long before he'd hugged her to death. Like everything
else in his kingdom, she'd become an object
of evaluation. Even the words he used to describe things
were like little boxes of confinement, little rocks
he threw at the moon, separating him further,
bringing him pieces, lodestones. And the guilt
of his isolation—he'd sworn off concubines,
it was that look in their far-off eyes, the crackling realization
reaching their minds that they'd been bought,
while he caressed the distant, perfect object in his hands.

He went often to the beach and stared like other people do
at the meditation before him.
The sun's long dangling finger across the water,
the honeyed line, shimmering like a zipper
on what he was coming to understand about it:
one conclusion, or another, here a god, there a god,
everywhere a god-god—he was aloofness itself,
and by that held the upper hand, the sponge,
squeezing it while soapy runs splattered

into gold chaos on the gray rocks; the servants
scrambled, able but wary, picking up his treasured flotsam.

Age made it worse. Aloha girls waved,
ever receding, their swaying hips
making the horizon like the hem of a grass skirt.
At least there was the gold. And he was the king,
king of the homunculus, giver of sciences,
wolfing down salad leaves before they lodged
in the back of his throat, cutting off fingernails,
letting them fall with a shrill clatter
onto the smooth golden floor which mirrored his feet.
He would cough, and wonder if his spray of golden spittle
would ignite the air into golden brightness
and make him fall with the last tinkling music
into the consummated, unabdicated otherness.

THREESOME

Paul does	whatever	Cat wants
whatever	Paul wants	Patti gets
Cat wants	Patti gets	Paul loves

Rachel Inez Lane

CATCH ME, ALFRED, I'M FALLING

Man, I could be a Hitchcock blonde. I'll have shades of white gloves
    lined up like criminals
on my dresser, wear them when I cup a man's face in my hands and hiss,
    Believe me.

Hitchcock blondes survive in the wild due to mirrors, and lips so red
    they stain sheets,
ties, love letters and breakup notes left on the table under the daisies
    next to the noose.

When I brush my hair I will be able to see my attacker out the corner
    of my vanity,
but since it's a false setup, he is now my lover, we'll have a picnic
    where I feed him

secret sandwiches on stiff stationery bread with Dior spread, straighten
    his lapel,
and sigh in his ear, *Let's go watch blah people through the binoculars.*

He'll stay up late drinking with cigarettes and undone ties, troubled by not
    knowing my
true story: How I grew up on a farm in Michigan where my father
    slaughtered pigs,

how my brother Theodore was oddly quiet and built bird houses. He won't
    know the tired smile
my mother would give after she broke the necks of chickens I named. He'll
    never know

how Hitchcock saw me in a Sears ad for dishwashers wearing my best
    oh, my! face,
my tricksy *mmm* face and flew in through my window, perched himself
    on my mantle

and taught me how to make a proper gimlet. We discussed Truffaut
    and the philosophy
of escaping in heels. He ordered me to write *I am Grace* in the air
    thirteen times with my foot.

Oh, I'd be a Hitchcock blonde with a pointy bra that could impale an infant's eye.
What a life it is to be seen from onyx angles, but under velvet lights, to hide clues

like the bubble gum inside my alligator purse. I'll peek through my glossy fingers,
watching as my man wrestles the killer to the ground, waiting for my cue

so I can start running to his musk, chin up, palms up and hair blowing
in the faint breeze of a fan a boy is hired to hold. A Hitchcock blonde who

dies elegant, because wouldn't it be sad to grow old in an A-line dress when you
look like a B or a D or worse, an O? I'd rather be lifted onto the gurney,
          practically

floating. Hitchcock watching as I am covered in a satin sheet. He's
          gnawing a cigar, holding
a lily, his arms around the sobbing boy with the fan, next to the brunette
          who scowls when

the EMT says, "My god, she's light as a ghost." Hitchcock replies, "Sir,
          she's no ghost
but an angel, a blonde, the best victim, like virgin snow that shows the bloody
          footprints."

Ken Letko

THE POWER OF LIGHT

can turn a white
dog black
a silhouette

on the horizon
sunlight unfolds
every new leaf

pulls a sumac
sprout through
four inches of asphalt

a red light stops a chain
of fast-moving cars
at an intersection

light you spend
all day every day
at the end of the tunnel

nine missing miners
on the windowsill
nine candles

widow's walk
a lantern for
a late boat

the moon
is your proxy
interrogating

the night sky
you can make
mud shine

any student
of the stars
knows the sky

can be any color

SALT

In this room down a hall
at the Hopewell House
every Wednesday
from 6:30 to 8:00 p.m.,
the widowed have agreed to meet
to lick the salt block.
My name tag reads
Albino deer (recessive rarity): widow at 35.
Dun-colored Helen and Marie
mistake me for a sheep or a goat
as we draw our chairs into a circle
of circumstance. Muscles in their aged faces
twitch with greed and suspicion.
In the larger world,
Jean and I would sit in adjoining streetcar seats,
read our newspapers,
and never share a headline.
Even Doris, who drags the remains
of a personal god at the bottom
of her purse, tucked next to non-prescription
reading glasses she bought on sale at Walmart,
shrinks from my pink eyes.
Louise has ten grandchildren,
three she and Harry were raising
because her daughter is, well, you know,
she doesn't want to say. She won't tell you either
that when Harry up and died like that,
some small part of her wished
he'd had the decency to take those kids with him,
but he never even took them to the park.
Betty lost a husband and found
a lump. Elsie says when the ambulance
comes to the Ridgewood Nursing Home,
they don't turn on the sirens
for fear they'll incite a riot
of dying. Ida says yeah, she knows.
She's lost two of them that way. I nod.
Judith's raised eyebrow asks
What could one with hooves so pale know of loss?
A marriage must be long
to be 40-years deep,
and grief is a black market business

best kept to themselves. If I taste it,
others will want it.
Young bucks will be dying in droves.
In war, in the streets,
in flaming buildings.
Or quietly in a bed next to me at night.
That sting in the wound, that particular tang
on the tongue, are theirs.
Keep me away from the salt.
Their old ones are sanctified,
their sorrow is sacred,
denial alive in the hide.

Marie-Elizabeth Mali

CAMPAIGN SEASON

We pray for the troops at war with old gear
in that intricate date-scented desert where
a mother spits. House and son gone this year.

Kill him, a man at the rally sneers,
as the first notes of "Strange Fruit" plummet the air.
We pray for the troops at war with old gear.

Jesus is hailed. Community organizers draw jeers.
Drill!, screeches the woman with upswept hair.
A mother spits. House and son gone this year.

A Kansas woman says it's Muslims she fears.
But they die in uniform for the ground we share.
We pray for the troops at war with old gear.

Wall Street and Main Street recklessly steer.
The story of a mother named Jocelyn Voltaire—
She spits. House foreclosed and son gone this year—

moves strangers to send $30K and volunteers.
The house stays hers for now, the court declares.
We pray for the troops at war with old gear.
A mother spits. House and son gone this year.

Kerrin McCadden

INTERSECTION

At the four-way stop I wave you on,
a kindness. You wave *no no, you go.* I wave, *go.*
We keep on. You insist. Me: *no you,*
please. A bird shifts, a sigh. The penned
horse tosses, pacing. I mouth *you go.*
There is a fleck on your windshield. I notice your hands.
Rain falls. Your hands cup the wheel
at ten o'clock and two, then float
past my knee and only sometimes land.
One hundred times on my back, they tame me.
Cars line up. Birds lift. I nod my head into your chest.
There is a trail of clothing. I walk to the
plank door of your room. This takes hours
and hours. This is a small cottage and there is sand
on the floor and nothing on the walls, crows calling,
dishes in the sink. Days go by. We are still making
our way to the bed. This is an inventory:
black telephone, board games, frayed chairs,
coffee table spotted with the old moons of drinks,
curtains pulled back on tiny hooks, single pane glass
windows like the ones I used to sneak out of at night, lifting
them as slow as this stepping, and when you talk
into my neck the words settle in the hammock
of my collarbone, puddle there and spill,
slide over my breasts and I am slowly covered,
and rinsed. I do not close my eyes. Nothing hurts.
The dust rises in swirls. Dogs bark. You turn
your windshield wipers on intermittent.
Your car rolls into the space I have built between us.
I am up to my belly in a northern lake, cold. I am afraid now.
When I get home, everyone will see.

Laren McClung

CONFLUENCE OF RIVERS AND MOUTHS

Today I saw a woman on Spring Street
with two black spaniels. She was crouching
and whispering to them. The dogs
took turns licking the woman on the mouth.
This woman's mouth was its own world.
There are many worlds. We can enter them.
I read that Frydek-Mistek is a natural gate
into the mountains. One river empties
into the mouth of another. I imagine you
singing your nightingale song back
in D.C. I forget little things. This is a way
of surviving. I make imprints in the snow
in my dreams aggressively, practice
my blues-scales, collapse bridges,
converse with my grandmother, walk
into the water and keep walking.
I don't know how surviving things can
better me, but I have many secrets.
And secrets, I'm learning, are like sheets,
or a shroud wrapped so tight it seems
impossible to find the opening to get out.

Sally Molini

MEAL TICKET

We've made the turkey's breast
so large it's an obstacle to mating,
the birds artificially imbued,
lots of creatures these days
needing an assist with things
they used to do for themselves.
No other earthlings consume as we do,
the planet's tender rotations
always tempting, commerce
done to a last turn. And the turkeys,
their so-called stupidity
a kind of innocence, stand in
crowded metal pens,
rain falling on those outside,
snoods and wattles trembling,
yellow bills turned up to sky
that once meant promise.
Instinct stirs, hope nesting
in a dark branch of cloud,
just enough to drown them.

FIXING CARS

I like the argument that man is alone in the universe,
and ipso facto its most intelligent being.
It proves there is no God, or if there is,
it's the god of low SAT scores.

Astronomers debate the dark matter between stars.
I picture a conversational pause with a Bush apologist,
each party wondering, What planet?

If I read the moon right tonight, there is no reading it.
If I tell my kid sister the stars are eyes twinkling,
why do their cold winks give me the shivers?

The smartest kid on our block couldn't jump-start
his engine if he was stuck in the wrong end of town
and his life depended on it. I can't read my tax form.
I fix his cars, he interprets the IRS,
and under Earth's starry hood,
we solve the problems of the universe.

Molly Peacock

A Tale of a T

T hurled itself down on the dry sweet grass
of the mowed orchard—part of its grandfather's lawn
—then lay on its back, looking up into
a latticework of branches for the first time.
(T had always thrown itself down to rest.
It was only ten, but walking seemed such an effort
—dragging around a whole decade!
But before T kept its nose in the green blades.)
One old tree arm above was shaggy and gray,
bearded with bark, studded with leaves

and the marble shapes of beginning apples.
Through the applets and leaves and bearded branch was sky
as blue as a bedroom wall.
The astonishing crisscrossing circles and lines
exploded into a pattern so unbearable
T had to close its eyes.
Yet the awe was still excruciating.
To relieve the pain, it painted letters, dry and sweet
on an imaginary tablet just overhead,
distracting itself with a word.

The one it chose—was it a choice, or a looming?
was lattice: two t's in the middle
and lattice is made of T's proliferating
just as the branches did.
An apple could hang on every t!
All of the ages of the world crossed above,
grandfather's bearded arm a branch
off the trunk... the trunk of... of life was a t:
from the infinity of the decade T had lived
it watched each apple increase into its girth,

the whole proliferating into lattice
while wonder whorled up like a fan blade,
and the world rose in its wind
and T rose
upright and at ease
beginning to walk toward the house
in search of a tablet
where it might write down
how it left the burden
of its decade on the ground.

Molly Peacock

THE SOFTIE

When there was something C wanted to say,
but he could only see it, not say it,
he'd tell his father,
"I can feel the answer in my mind,"
—and he could, soft and oily as lamb's wool—
"but I don't know the words for it."
Then you don't know the answer, Capital C would say.
You don't have an idea except in words.
Yet C did too have an idea,
soft and unformed as a penis on a sleeping boy.

Years later, on the phone to her, his father
crept into his mind: *No ideas but as words.* "Ohhh,"
C whispered into the satin-edged blanket of nothingness,
"Ohhh, I love you." That was not really his idea.
In his mind it was much more complex,
and had as many spinnings to it as twists in yarn.
He'd knit up his thought too early.
I love you really were the wrong words to say,
for his longing was vague and curled,
and the three words stood for three thousand,
and fell as three boy warriors, sacrificed for an army of 3,000
who stayed asleep in their tents.

So she took it wrong. Thought her hard thought,
something capitalized instantly,
a suit.

Later excuses of a nameless nature were made
and avoidances,
nothing either had words for,
something the Couples Counselor could never unravel.
But from that old moment of false commitment,
C felt the value of his silences.
He was a soft C,
while Capital C had been hard,
and his son's mother, his ex-wife, was hard.

Even as a grandfather with a rumpled blanket of a face
C often did not bother to speak.
Saying things killed them.
Why would a person want to close up a thought?

Why not leave things open,
and receive?
Then he hooked his grandchild under his arm
and carried him up to bed
with his son walking upstairs beside them.
Tucking the boy in after grandpa left, his son explained,
Oh Big C, he's a softie. He never says nothing.

J. F. Quackenbush

To a Child
for Stella March Faiello

I hope that you are beautiful
and that your eyes are green
and your hair is blonde.

I hope that you are loved
and cared for. I hope your
life as you come into it
is not a field of broken things.

I hope that you are smart
and funny, and a goddess of words
that will spill from your lips
in this language
that is the only lover I have left.

I hope that the sadness
this awfulness now that surrounds
your conception does not print
itself in your face so that you
are born hating the way only
those of us like you and I
who are children of injustice
can hate.

I hope your father is a good man
and he manages to love your mother
like I did, unworthy of it as she is.

I hope that in another few decades
you are not sitting drunk and numb
dead inside and staring down at your
typing fingers from 10,000 feet above yourself
writing words like these on an empty page.

To the child I will never know,
I might have loved you; you could have
been mine. If you were a boy, your
name would be Fyodor.
I like to think I would have named you Chloe.
Or Theresa.

If you hear her say anything about me
see my name on the spine of a book
find an old letter that I've signed
or poem that I've written, don't ask her
who I am. Just wait.

A time will come when she will look
at you, into your red rimmed eyes
after your heart has been broken
by a boy who reminds her of herself.

And when she does, your eyes, just
a little like mine, will make her
think of me, and she'll crumble
a little at the memory of how she
came to have you and all the love
that came into the world in your
tiny infant fingers reaching for
her breast.

That's how you will know me,
in the reflection in her eyes
watching the ghost of me
drown quietly in your tears.

Rebekah Remington

HAPPINESS SEVERITY INDEX

Though in the lower standard deviation, I fall, the statistician says,
within the normal range of happiness. Therefore, no drugs today.

What about tomorrow? What if doodling stars isn't enough?
Will I be asked to color the rainbow one more time?

Name three wishes that might come true?
List everything I've been given within a minute?

Though within the normal range of happiness, I score poor
on bird appreciation, poor on oboe joy. My responses, in fact,

seem to indicate an overall confusion concerning joy itself.
What did I mean that during parties I choose the sofa

like a sick cat? That when tattoos are dispensed I'm first
in line? That books full of other people's misery make

the beach infinitely more pleasant? Stargazing is another weakness.
Too much I examine the patch of dirt where nothing grows

where buried curiosa aren't deep enough, though in Short Answer
I say I'm not in favor of frequent masturbation. Friends call.

Mostly the machine answers. Mozart makes me cry.
I kill spiders without guilt. To make up for this

I take the kids to the golden arches play area.
A positive indicator. Also, interest in the existential

is minimal. I approve of make-up and ice cream.
When I wake early, I get out of bed. When I wallow

in planetary counterpoint, it never lasts. And here's what
really saves me: if I were a ghost I'd be Casper. If I were a tradition

I'd be a dreidel. I like the rain. I like the rain. When the boat drifts off
I wave. When the dog runs off I follow.

David Romtvedt

ON BROADWAY

My Uncle Will wanted to be on Broadway.
After family dinners, when everyone sat around
drinking coffee, he'd do a little tap dance or shuffle.
Of course it was embarrassing to have a grown man
who worked at the lumberyard dancing after dinner.

On my ninth birthday, I became his reluctant partner.
We wore white shirts, red jackets, and black patent
leather shoes he'd bought at the Salvation Army Thrift Shop
along with paper top hats from the party supply store
and canes made from PVC tubing he'd painted gold.
Our big number was "Putting on the Ritz."

The other day I looked up in the sky and saw Uncle Will
floating in an aluminum lawn chair. He leaned forward
and grabbed a bit of cloud that was shaped like a woman.
I don't remember him as a lady's man so maybe
I invented the woman. She was wearing a tutu
but moved more like a stripper than a ballerina.
Uncle Will was whistling Broadway tunes and talking
to himself about the right expression and inflexion
to impress a casting director at an audition.

Then my aunt, his wife Jane, came into the sky.
She was carrying drinks and a plate of strawberries
and whipped cream, the same as in real life.
Sometimes when we finished, Aunt Jane would look
at Uncle Will, a dark sympathetic look, and she'd say,
"Will, if you worked hard you could still audition."
The way he looked back at her—even now floating
in the sky—it's a good thing angel uncles don't carry guns.
"Oh, I don't know," he'd say, too casually.
"I can't give up the lumberyard."

I look again and realize my Uncle Will was afraid.
I never knew. When the song ends, we tap the edges
of our paper top hats with our PVC canes and bow
and everyone claps like mad, Jane most of all.

Ralph James Savarese

NOR YET A DREAM OF WAR

For Kevin, the former Defense Secretary's son

We were sixth-graders at middle school camp,
conscripts in an old regime of the masculine,

privates third-class,
dreading the common shower,

the inevitable comparisons—
my own genital region like an unplanted field

far from a forest.
We didn't much care for our unit,

especially the bigger boys, lords of the rise
they got out of you,

bullies snapping their towels,
giving someone a wedgie.

Two hours into the trip and you were miserable:
a sullen lump on the rope swing.

The second night, after the ghost stories
and guitar, after the game

of capture the flag,
after the Walton family imitations

("Night, John Boy. Night, Mary Ellen"),
you showed up at my bed—unannounced,

shivering, distraught.
"I'm cold," you whispered, tapping me

on the shoulder. "I'm cold."
And I, drowsy with sleep,

thinking you were my baby sister
scared of a thunderstorm,

or not thinking at all, told you
to crawl in.

℅ ℞

And that's how, the next morning,
the gym teacher found us:

in the same zipped-up sleeping bag,
the same sweaty, blue cocoon of dreams.

Remember trying to scramble back to consciousness?
Suddenly, a voice loud enough to wake

the other boys:
"WHAT ARE YOU TWO DOING?"

Like a street urchin flushed from an underground city,
you maneuvered through winding

passageways and inky, muck-filled sewers
to locate a manhole.

Then lifting the cumbersome lid,
you rose into shame—I right behind you.

℅ ℞

Say we were two boys together clinging
(that's how Whitman once put it),

two boys wrapped in goose-feather affection,
our skulls propped against one another

like pick-up sticks, sunlight
pouring into the musty cabin, splashing

on the walls—dawn once again at it
with her water canon.

All that muscle-crowned gym teacher
could talk about was sex

and a word (sodomy) we didn't understand.
His fellow chaperone, the guidance counselor,

insisted on phoning our fathers.
"What they need is a good man-to-man."

Yours was hysterical—let us say,
representatively so.

Three tears for the moderate Republican
from Maine, that toupee-ed paradox!

He saw the future as a carpet at last unrolled,
a red one ruined by moths.

So much for ever being President...
Mine, the corporate lawyer,

made a motion
to hold me in contempt.

                        ℘ ℭ

Must a boy swim upstream for miles and then
like a salmon agreeably die?

What has become of you,
my disconsolate bedmate?

Are you able to follow the federal guidelines
on loneliness,

that preposterous compromise?
You can *be* lonely,

but you can't tell anyone,
nor can anyone ask.

If I had to guess: you're probably married now
with children,

an amiable enough, country-club sort
of citizen, a lobbyist or defense contractor

preaching the gospel of national security
while taking advantage of Pop's

incomparable connections.
(The old man like a base-runner

stranded at third,
having made it to congressman, then senator,

then the loyal opposition's
Pentagon head.)

℘ ☙

Last night I saw your father,
the now former Secretary, on television.

He's been hired as a commentator
for the upcoming war.

"Soon, a squadron of bombers will swoop down
over Baghdad," he reported, "dropping

their loads, doing their dirty business
in the dark." Well,

he didn't say that exactly,
though his enthusiasm *was* nearly sexual.

America has begun its chant;
outside, even the cicadas are preparing

for combat, pounding their thoraxes.
In the first Gulf conflict,

pilots were given pornographic materials
as a motivational tool.

"Go out and give it to her," the men joked
as they climbed up to their cockpits.

Then lifting the cumbersome lids,
they rose into shame—

the entire country behind them.
So many miles, so much distance.

Look, the dead crawl into their body bags
alone. Remember playing

beneath the streets? Remember the warmth
of my breath on your shoulder?

There wasn't a girl between us
nor yet a dream of war.

Lauren Schmidt

GRANDMA ZOLIE GIVES UNHEEDED ADVICE

If ever your husband comes home drunk, don't
beat him while he sleeps; you'll just end up confessing to it.

If ever you drive your car up on the curb, don't
keep it a secret; your son will find out when he sees
the tires wobbling and will be sore when he learns
it's actually the second time.

If ever you want to teach your grandchildren not to smoke, don't
flash them your pneumonectomy scars or wag the rubber-insert
breast in their face. It will scare the bejeezus out of them.

(If ever you want to make them laugh, though,
spit your dentures in the meatloaf.)

If ever you can't finish your dinner, don't save the leftovers.
They'll just lodge in your freezer for six months until

you can stand to throw them away. But don't throw things away.
Fix them, mend, reuse them, clean them, and that goes for you too.
You don't want to be the smelly grandmother, for Heaven's sake.

If ever your grandson tells a joke with the word *queef* in it,
don't repeat, for clarification, *Pussy fart?* when he answers you.

Which brings me to swearing. If ever you need to swear, don't
take the Lord's name, say *shugamaloot* instead, or,
if you have to swear, say *shit-fuck-goddammit* like a lady,

because when a nurse instructs your stroke-stricken husband
to shit in his bed, you'll want to have something to say.

If ever you're mad at the family who is mad at you
for christening the neighbor's baby in the bathroom, don't
threaten to stop taking your meds: it only works the first time.

If ever you're about to die, don't ask the Lord for more time,
because the Lord is good and He just might give it to you.

Mather Schneider

BETWEEN US AND IT

I'm a white American and she's Mexican
but we're trying to make it work.
We've moved in together.
There's a dumpster outside our bedroom window
15 feet away,
a cement block wall
between us and it,
a gray cement block wall that's full of air
and means nothing.
The dumpster belongs to the other apartment building,
the last of the expensive white ones
before it turns Mexican.
At night me and my girlfriend
are frightened by people
throwing things into the dumpster.
The noises are sudden and vicious, like thunder
or war, as if they are so proud,
as if it was the surest thing in the world
to be throwing away a microwave at midnight.
Later in the night we hear the Mexicans
taking things out of the dumpsters
to fix and resell.
The nights are hot in the desert in the summer
and in our sweaty sleep
the blanket on the bed gets pushed
and mashed together
between us.
We call it "the border."
Even on the hottest nights we can't
toss it away.

Prartho Sereno

ELECTRODOMESTICO

One day the iceman came no more.
Neither did the coalman with his telescopic chute.
Nor the junkman with his horse and cart,
his dust and sweat-streaked face.
Not even the milkman's xylophone
of bottles could be heard jangling
through the magenta streets of dawn.

That day the wide-eyed band of women
in calico aprons, pockets bulging with
clothespins, were swept away to a buzzing
world where everything came with its own
complication of cord. But these women of faith
knew what to do. They dove in and took refuge
in Houdini's secret, hiding a small brass key
in their mouths.

And they did what they'd always done,
took everyone in—the plug-in refrigerator
and washing machine, a menagerie of electric
can openers, ice-crushers, and coffee mills.
And the Edsel of home appliances:
the sit-down steam press that could snatch
a shirt from your hands, send it back
an origami waffle with melted buttons.

It was Fat Tuesday in the history of man's
imagination, a festival of dazzling inventions,
each one out-doing the next. The bobby pin
bowed to the Spoolie, the Spoolie
to the electric roller. The wood-sided
station wagon sidled up, wired
with a radio and its very own garage.

And the suburbs—that great yawn of grass
with its pastel stutter of houses, all
stocked with friendly products: Hamburger
Helper, Aunt Jemima, a detergent
called Cheer, a dish soap named Joy.
Turquoise linoleum nests, feathered
with vim and verve where they delivered
us, girls who grew into flowers, ceding

ourselves to the wind. They watched
in dismay as we pulled up those tender
roots and headed out for the likes of India
or Back to the Land. They couldn't understand
why we left our humming dowries behind—
plug-in frying pans, carving knives, and brooms.

But on our way out they drew near,
as mothers do, and slipped us the keys—
the small brass keys they'd kept all the while
in their mouths, but never used.

Lee Sharkey

BERLIOZ

Now let us praise Hector Berlioz
who found himself one night composing
a symphony as he slept who woke
lucid remembering the entire
first movement in A minor he could
have sat down at his desk and begun
transcribing as during the first hours
after a great destruction we see
in detail each small thing that was lost
as after my house went up in flames
carrying with them all of my poems
I sat on a mattress on a cold
floor and began to reconstruct them
found I could remember all of them
if only the night were long enough
but Berlioz willed himself not to
pick up his pen his wife was ill if
he wrote the first notes he knew himself
too well for months nothing would exist
except poured silver he would not write
the articles that sustained them how
would he pay for her medicine how
would he buy food he willed himself not
to pick up the pen yet the next night
the symphony visited him once
more it called him to service it called
him to adoration it took all
his strength to lie back down until he
finally fell asleep and the spurned
muse left him just as I fell asleep
laying my head on my journal and
the poems I had not transcribed left me
with only my child and my mate and
the spring where I knelt and chopped through ice
to draw the blessing of water let
us praise Berlioz for his unsung
symphony of medicine and bread

06.25.00 – PHiSH – ALLTEL PAVILION, NC

                                    Left
                                    side:
                                    mystified
                                    stoners "Oh
                    my   G!d" our
                    heroine—   Khaki-hat
    frat   bros toss   bottle caps
      in   from the   right: Set
    break   on lawn   at summer
    show,   Fishman's   side. 25,000
      spent the   last hour-   ten giggin'-out
      dancing: N.I.C.U.,   *Sample in a Jar,*
      Old Home   *Place, P.Y.*   *I.T.E., Water*
      in the Sky,   *Funky Bitch,*   *Horn, Heavy*
      Things, Dirt,   *Split Open & Melt*—and now,
      Jeff & Bones   are mind-goners: all gooball
      body-highed   up and in right behind:
      chopped-up   black hair dyed red—
      dyed raver   bright inferno-red: no-
      kidding   lip-ringed candy   flip,
      neon pop-   plastic bracelets,   glittery
        skin—and   she's not just masturbating:
            Lying down,   she's full-on/head-back/back-
          arched slapping herself—down in her patch-
          work, rub/stroke/moan/oh-slapping with
          what looks like the multiple arms of Kali   Ma—
          And, with whatever it is that's on her, rubies trolling/
          showing the hold, she's upside-down staring at/into
    Jeff   as if he were Shiva, about to be ferociously dom-
  inated.   —Quartet returns, crowd erupts, *Gotta Jibboo*
  opens   second set: The whatever-you-want-it-to-mean
    melody stands her up, CK5's lightshow coats her skin in bouncing   blue
    and off comes her top; braless breasts are hers to fondle. Ev'ryone around's
      gaping, dancers having serious difficulties: "—Make her stop!" a girl
        cries "—Somebody do something!" But then screw all that: She
          wants it—Kali Ma's back on her back, arches, yes, eyes,
      Jeff, again groans to town slapping herself like a
          bass guitar, uproariously finishes off and
          passes out, topless. Guy to the
          right goes, "M'm, yer
          sumthin special,
          ain't cha?"
        and two
from the left get security.

Charlie Smith

THE CASING

For years I sat in bars lying about everything,
concealing my limp, offering vinyl
suitcases for sale and proposing to women
who'd overlooked themselves. I gave away

folding tables and threatened
species like lopsided turtles and misused
harness bulls. I wasn't as speedy as I claimed to be
or as galled by those without

a purpose in life. I sold three-day
vacations to resorts that existed
only in your mind. I liked to watch the breeze
take leafy boughs in hand.

The limits to man's ability
to reach the stars were no problem for me.
I sank my nose in foreign papers
looking for tiny lots I might build

my dream house on. I said I owned
hotels and racks for smoking arctic char.
I claimed to notice something burning
in the kitchen. A leaf seemed at times to urge

a change in plans. Probably the winds
were coming from the east. I gave away
my watch and told the time by the degradation
of building materials. I spelled the stuporized.

The sun, an old friend, eased
onto the brickyard wall. I sensed an era
drawing to a close. Something told me,
so I said, to gather up my things. Smoothed-

over ideas, frets, a capacity for change
unremarked on by others, a boarding house
menu I used for a text, my bindle, palpebral musings,
a burial suit of lights

and a jar of brandied apricots—all these
I said I'd send a van back for and never did.

S-Plan

Bacon Academy
Colchester, CT
October 31st, 2001

1.

Shortly after 9/11,
a boy who had been stealing pick-up trucks
from a local dealership
and hiding them in the woods
so he could sell them later,
decided to fashion a fake bomb
and place it on the loading dock
outside the cafeteria
on Halloween morning.

We, of course, were all still
emotionally threadbare
and sent into a frazzle.

The first order of the morning
was to stop the buses
before they got into the parking lot,
and not let the kids into the school.

As each top-heavy yellow clunker
pulled its plume of blue smoke into the drive,
we stopped it and tried to explain
what was going on,
without freaking out the vampires,
witches, monsters, and ghosts,
12 buses,
each filled with high school kids
all being something else for the day.

We sent the buses to the elementary school,
where all 800 ghouls
would hang out in the tiny gym
until the danger had passed.

Take a moment here to imagine that.

2.

I thought of my own youth—
different time, same fear—
the old days of "duck and cover,"
air raid horn baying at the spring sky,
and all of us either balled up under our desks,
or standing, boy girl boy girl
against the cool, cool
painted cinder block walls
in the shadowy hallways of St. Mary's,
the perfume of lilacs
in the breeze that breathed there,

or before me, in England,
the shelters in underground tubes,
railway arches, subways,
and my Auntie Elsie,
staring in dread at the ceiling
in the shelter in her cellar.

And later,
after the Russians did their bomb,
and Yuri Gagarin swirled around in our sky,
General Foods and General Mills
sold dried war rations,
and the nuclear protection suit was a hot item.

Wall Streeters even claimed
that the bomb shelter business
would gross billions in the coming years,
if there were any.
And every day
the radio sizzled warnings
that a shoddy, homemade shelter
would get you broiled "to a crisp"
or squeezed "like grapefruit,"
as in American neighborhoods
people built "wine cellars,"
or else the contractors worked
under cover of night.

I cried into our couch
for 14 days straight in 1962,

and I didn't even really know why
beyond the fact that all the adults
seemed quiet and scared,
and I understood the word annihilation,
and saw, over and over again,
the documentary where the house
gets blown away sideways
by a speeding cloud of nuclear winter.

But the bomb never fell,
even though everyone,
including me,
kept fear in their hearts,
and spent years
practicing for the end,

3.

and it's the same now.

When the kids returned to school
later that morning,
we tried to resume a
typical Halloween
in a typical American high school,
the kids dressed to kill,
the sugar-high higher
because they were back on familiar ground.
But the party didn't last long.

Soon a voice filled with urgency
squawked over the perpetual loudspeaker
that we needed to immediately
go into the "S-plan."

Ignore all fire alarms and bells.

Students in the hallway
should run to the nearest classroom.

Teachers lock your classroom door.

Do not let ANYONE in.

If students ask to be let in,
do not let them in.
Direct them to the office.
Do not let them in.

Cover the windows
with the black paper
that you've put aside
for this occasion.

Huddle all your students
into the corner,
away from the windows and doors.

Do not use the school phone
or your cell phone.

Stay there until you receive instructions.

And we did. For two hours,
me and the bum,
the Ninja Turtle,
the Queen of Hearts,
fear in the eyes behind the masks,
fear in the tears of the ballerina.

Arthur Vogelsang

ENVIRONMENTAL

Unfortunately rather than grass there was white paste
Or rather than an orange tiger lily there was white white out,
And a lime tree or an outfield? No instead there was white medicine
In a normal tube which over and over had to refill
Itself to cover the whole major league outfield
And on nice brown and black checked sheets with brown pillowcases
There were without mercy each night snow and white glue mixed
With snow in my spot in the bed.
In the morning, we fully awake, the glue was fifty percent
Of the snow that was shoveled from the walk. Each day such snow
Was waiting outside and of each day the first five hours
I shoveled. Tell me yours.

OK. The pets whose names you know well were dead, all fourteen,
The ones who are six years old and the ones who are fifty-two,
Or they were all lost, we could not find out *which it was*. The people
We know, or knew (and that's the hard part)
Were also hopefully lost rather than decayed
With no consciousness, and we searched for the creatures and humans
Every waking minute in the endless cities then went to sleep
And as we slept we hoped they were hopelessly lost not dead.

David Wagoner

BEFORE THE POETRY READING

They've left me standing in the hall, alone,
outside the room where I'm going to put myself
and some poems on display. The man in charge
is making sure the microphone is too short
and the table holding the lectern has one leg
just short enough.
             I shouldn't be nervous now
(though I used to watch my teacher, Theodore Roethke,
throw up before readings), and why did I remember
Stanley Kunitz telling me he'd searched
through almost a whole Animal Husbandry Building,
up and around and down stairs and more stairs
before a reading, hunting a men's room
so he wouldn't disgrace American poetry
onstage in public? He finally found a door
in a dark basement labeled SWINE.
                     I'm trying
to think of almost anything other than
what's about to happen. Tonight's hallway
belongs to Natural History. Behind my back
they've stuffed a display case full of local birds
on glass shelves, all of them glassy-eyed,
staring at me and past me at late arrivals
who are mostly polite enough not to stare back
at birds like us, though some give a quick glance,
embarrassed, as if they were going to flunk
Advanced Ornithology.
             A golden plover,
a marsh hawk, a bluejay, a saw-whet owl, and a raven
beside me are posed and poised to defend themselves
against all those inside their critical distance.
From an unlabeled doorway, my keeper beckons.

Mike White

NASCAR

Not rolling in liquid fire
or pulled apart by physics.
Not between commercials.

But the way an old dog
half-blind
noses around and around

some quiet
apple-scented
chosen ground.

Jeff Worley

LUCKY TALK

> *"I think poems are pieces of talk, savored and sustained.*
> *I would call them 'lucky talk.'"*
> —William Stafford, "A Witness for Poetry"

Yesterday at Kroger, I heard a boy, maybe 7,
say to his father: *We have two eyes and two arms*
and two legs. Why don't we have two penises?
I love language most when it slips up on us like this.

Which is why, of course, poets sneak up their ears
in cafes and bars. *I've never done that*
with anybody, and I'm certainly not going to
do it with you, I heard, unmoored from its context,

as I pretended to study Pazzo's menu.
And later that same lucky day: *Jonathan's*
not a bad person really; he's just insufferable.
My wife, always the dutiful daughter, brought

her mother a bright Sunday bouquet.
These flowers are so beautiful, she said,
they look artificial. And my favorite,
from Luis Polonia on ESPN after being traded

from New York: *The Yankees are interested*
in only one thing, and I don't know what that is.

2009
RATTLE POETRY PRIZE
$5,000 WINNER

photo by Matt Phillips

LYNNE KNIGHT
Berkeley, CA

for

"TO THE YOUNG MAN WHO CRIED OUT 'WHAT WERE YOU THINKING?' WHEN I BACKED INTO HIS CAR"

In *The Music of Poetry*, T. S. Eliot wrote that, "while poetry attempts to convey something beyond what can be conveyed in prose rhythms, it remains, all the same, one person talking to another." The argument was for the use of common speech, but the concept contains much more than that. A powerful poem focuses its immediacy and intensity into an overwhelming presentness, the consuming sense that everything is happening *now*; through direct address a poet is able to speak to us all. So when Lynne Knight responds to the man who cried out in insensitivity, it's a response to the lack of compassion everywhere, and a communion with those who've experienced it on both sides. If poetry can change the world, this is the kind of poetry that can, one small act at a time. For this reason, and others, we're proud to introduce "To the Young Man Who Cried Out..." as winner of the 2009 Rattle Poetry Prize.

Lynne Knight

TO THE YOUNG MAN WHO CRIED OUT "WHAT WERE YOU THINKING?" WHEN I BACKED INTO HIS CAR

I was thinking No. No, oh no. Not one more thing.
I was thinking my mother, who sat rigid
in the passenger seat crying, *How terrible!*
as if we had hit a child not your front bumper,
would drive me mad, and then there would be
two of us mad, mother and daughter, and things
would be easier, they said things would be easier
once she went to the other side, into complete total
madness. I was thinking how young you looked,
how impossibly young, and trying to remember
myself young, my body, my voice, almost another
person, and I wanted to weep for all I had let
come and go so casually, lovers, cities, flowers,
and then I was thinking *You little shit* for the way
you stood outside my window with your superior air
as if I were a stupid old woman with a stupid old woman
beside her, stood shouting *What were you thinking?*
as if I were incapable of thought, as I nearly was,
exhausted as I'd become tending my mother,
whom I had just taken to the third doctor in so many
days, and you shouting your rhetorical question
then asking to see my license, *your li-cense,* slowly,
as if I would not understand the word, and the lover
who made me feel as if I never knew anything
appeared then, stepped right into your body saying
What were you thinking? after I had told him, sobbed
to him, that I thought he was, I thought he was,
I thought we would—and then my mother began
to cry, as if she had stepped into *my* body, only years
before, or was it after, and suddenly I saw the whole
human drama writ plain, a phrase I felt I had never
understood until then, an October afternoon in Berkeley,
California, warm, warm, two vehicles stopped in
heavy traffic on campus, a woman deciding to make way
for a car trying to cross Gayley, act of random kindness
she thought might bring her luck then immediately—
right before impact—knew would be bad luck,
if it came, being so impure in its motive,
and then the unraveling of the beautiful afternoon
into anger and distress that would pass unnoticed
by most of the world, would soon be forgotten by those

witnessing the event, and eventually those experiencing it
while the sun went on lowering itself toward the bay
and gingko trees shook their gold leaves loose
until a coed on the way home from class, unaware
a car had backed into another car, unaware of traffic,
stopped to watch the shower of gingko, thought of Zeus
descending on the sleeping Danaë in a shower of gold,
and smiled over all her own lover would do
in the bright timeless stasis before traffic resumed.

Michelle Bitting

MAMMARY

Hawks circle fields near the highway
homing in to catch the scent
of animals deep in the high dry grass.
So many wildflowers in bloom,
watery purples and acid yellows,
I'm dizzy in my car
blazing up the California coast:
Santa Barbara, Pismo, Salinas,
nicknamed *The salad bowl of the world*
with its patchwork plots
of endive and spinach,
the almighty artichoke
in whose honor Norma Jean Baker
was once crowned queen.
So fresh in her red gingham blouse,
remember? Her elation,
her perky, generous D cups
held up to the leafy bulbs
as everyone cheered. If only
it stayed so rosy, the tough layers
unstripped, the heart left intact.
If only you weren't topless
on a gurney, Rachel,
under the scouring glare
of hospital lights,
your own sweet breasts
offered up to the surgeon's blade.
A hundred miles north
of where you are right now
I'm a slave to this shifting view,
anything to avoid the thought
of your chest picked clean,
tender globes that fed three mouths,
now poison the body's crop.
So I'll imagine birds and flight
as the elliptical sweep of sharpness
cuts the pale sky of your chest,
steel beaks of surgical tools
carving out the flesh cream,
making smoke of tumor meat—say goodbye,
pay my respects
and picture them floating up,

slipping through the ceiling cracks,
two blond angels,
flying out
beyond the moon's milky scar,
they spread their innocence
over the lustrous scrim of L.A.,
those brave, radiant girls
wave and then they're gone.

Mary-Lou Brockett-Devine

CRABS

The only thing I know
is they can crawl, swim,
and bite like hell.
        —*"Chas" Howard*
            in Beautiful Swimmers

And this, then, is the wonder of evolution:
crabs cannot fly. Imagine them
with their five pairs of legs (eight for walking,
two adapted into claws) hovering over
your family picnic, piercing the skin
of your hotdog as you duck their armored
dives or working in flocks to carry off
a roasted chicken or your tabby cat. What kind
of collar would dogs wear to repel these bugs
with shells so thick it takes a hammer

to crack their claws, a hatchet to hack them
in half to bait a blackfish hook? Calico
crabs, kelp crabs, and king crabs with claws
that can reach to pinch flesh no matter where
you hold them. Box crabs, rock crabs, and spider
crabs, so wiry they could land on your head
and wrap their long legs around your chin—
their wild wings keeping tension on your jaw
as the claws try to rip off something soft. What hope
for the songbirds? Crabs in the branches

plucking featherless chicks from the nest
like oysters on the half shell. Crabs lifting lids,
picking scraps from the trash cans, clinging
to power lines, scavenging road kill, clacking up
the sides of brick buildings, the tips
of their sharp toes scraping at your screens
on August nights. Red crabs, green crabs,
blue crabs—so bright, children
will think them beautiful the way
they think flames are flowers until

they reach plump fingers to the stove. Crabs
from every ocean, eyes adapted to bright
light as they learn to live like their cousins

the land crabs—dry with only shallow puddles
to drink from—then migrating inland,
burying themselves in damp ground to rest,
waiting to spring up and grab anything
(bare toes, dog's paw) that puts pressure
on their underground beds. Baby
crabs hatching from jellied eggs, scuttling

across sidewalks, scurrying through parking lots
into back yards and cellars, where they squeeze out
of that first shed shell, spread their new-found wings,
and fly. So tonight, as you tuck the sheet beneath
your chin, give thanks that the winged things
that draw blood tend to be small enough to crush.
That the winged things with claws tend to eat seed.
And that the crabs still cling to the rocks beneath
the water, as they wave their stiff claws above their heads
drawing slow circles around the dim and distant stars.

Carolyn Creedon

HOW TO BE A COWGIRL IN A STUDIO APARTMENT

> *Paint the ceiling blue and let it dry. See pamphlet "How to Paint a*
> *Ceiling." Chalk a large circle to represent the sun. A light bulb will*
> *do as well. Start close to the sun and trace Mercury. Trace each*
> *planet. Finish with Pluto. Pour each color into a plastic container.*
> *Paint each planet and the sun.*
> > *—from anonymous pamphlet, "How to Paint*
> > *the Solar System on Your Ceiling"*

Don't let the people at Ace Hardware tell you you need a man.
Do pick one up anyway, if he looks red and ripe. A cowgirl needs
nourishment, and some nights, to lie on her back and let something
bloom above her, looming like the stars. A cowgirl's hardware
is indispensable—big-spurred boots, canteen, and a saddle to go—
useful, but always that soft underbelly she won't be revealing.
No need for the little black dress: a flannel shirt, jeans, a steaming
pan of wieners, and some bourbon. And him, over there. *"Hey You!"*
He'll come over. He'll have to. You're a renegade, a rough ride, a rogue feeling.
Paint the ceiling blue and let it dry. See pamphlet "How to Paint a Ceiling."

Get him there. Rein him in a little; don't let him roam too much.
You're well-schooled in herding. Circle him, if you must, with a lasso,
then lead him—carry him, if you must, over one shoulder—over
his objections, over a bottle of wine, to the bed. Make him docile.
Hum like a whittled banjo. It helps if you know how to pet a wild
animal, or how to rub two sticks together with your hands, or shell
peanuts husk by husk—cowgirl skills that will come in handy when
rustling up blades of grass to whistle on, or handling unpredictable
forces that scare so easily. Undo his fly. Make him rise and swell.
Chalk a large circle to represent the sun. A light bulb will do as well.

Remember, he's borrowed, cowgirl; you don't buy things, the stars
you ride under slide over you like yellow peanuts, the big sky just
a rented ceiling, the big sun a borrowed bulb, a giant library card
from God. The planets unmoored are not your marbles, and the warm
man you rolled with, rode and sweated with, will go back to his natural
habitat, glistening wet. This is your rule: the cowgirl's status quo.
Bowls are only good for what they hold, branches for the scratch they
itch, stones for chalking circles of the light. Even your rope just
rings out the moon, your banjo mouth twangs out a temporary tempo.
Start close to the sun and trace Mercury. Trace each planet. Finish with Pluto.

Mark out the man. Trace him with your tongue like an outline of the moon made of milk. You're a cowgirl. Circle him like you would a wild bull in a cloud of red dust. Then let your wanting run, turn it over like a bucket of color, let it spill into the other, and, panting, let it dry until it's done. Then let him go. Untie the steed, neighing softly and nosing the shag-carpet tumbleweeds beneath the semi-glossed glow. Mosey into the kitchenette, holster your gun. Ride the man gently back home, to whatever field or farm or store you stole him from. Leave him there, with the other sticky objects: the marbles, the broken-up pieces of stars, the rolling painting circles, fading into sky, one by one. *Pour each color into a plastic container. Paint each planet and the sun.*

Douglas Goetsch

WRITER IN RESIDENCE, CENTRAL STATE

I'm writing this from nowhere. Oklahoma
if you care. It's not south, not west, not really
Midwest. Think of a hairless Chihuahua
on the shoulder of Texas, make an X,
I'm in the middle, in an apartment
above the dumpsters on a parking lot
across from a football stadium.
The shriveled leaves of what passes
for autumn scuttle across the blacktop.
Prairie Striders stand under cars saying *Hey
fuck you* to French pluperfects in the pines.
I've renamed the birds. They don't seem to mind.
In Oklahoma when you say a word
like *pluperfect*, somehow you're certain
no one in the state has used it that day.

Sometimes the parking lot feels like a lake,
a lake with light towers and cars on top of it.
Sometimes I see an Indian burial ground
under there. You don't think of asphalt as earth,
but if they paved the entire prairie—which
seems to be the plan—it would still curve
with the horizon and shine in the sun.
And no matter where you are, if you let
the world quiet down you'll start to hear
the most terrible things about yourself.
But then, like a teenager, it'll tire of cursing
and deliver you into the silence of graves.
You'll look out on the world and see
yourself looking out. Now I know
when monks retreat to the charnel ground
and stay there long enough, the demons
tire of shouting. No battles, no spells: you wait
for them to cry themselves to sleep.

If everyone were healed and well
and all neuroses gone, would there
be anything left to write about?
Maybe just weather and death.
I'd like to die on a mountain in winter
in New Hampshire, the one the old man
climbed, having decided his natural time

was done. How alive he must have been
during that short series of lasts—last step,
last look around, bend of the waist,
head on the ground, the soundless closing
of his lids. How easy to be in love
with the earth, breathing the crystalline air
as he shivered and yawned
and let the night take him home.

Back in New York City there's a book
of Freud high on a shelf that presided
over far too much. *The past,* it kept
insisting, *the past.* There was also a mouse,
who came out whenever I was still
and quiet for long enough. She'd sniff
my foot, go to the floor-length mirror,
then drag her long tail into the kitchen.
At first I set a trap. Then I knew her
to be the secret life of my apartment,
witness to everything without comment,
her visit my reward for keeping still,
for praying in a closet as Jesus advised.

Don't worry, said a woman last winter.
I can see you're worried. She had the wrinkled
eyes of an old Cherokee, and spoke of past
lives without a trace of contrivance.
The silence here on weekends is so total
it holds me. Even when the stadium
is full, I don't hear the people, just the PA
telling who tackled who—who in Oklahoma
was born and raised and fed and coached
to deliver a game-saving hit. I don't
know where I will be or what I will do
next year, but five miles underground
in the womb of the earth there is
no money, no lack of money, no decisions
about dinner or weekends, friends
or enemies, no stacks of unanswered mail.
I'm trying to live there, so I can live here.

David Hernandez

REMEMBER IT WRONG

Everyone's memory is subjective. If in three weeks we
were both interviewed about what went on here
tonight, we would both probably have very, very
different stories.
> —*James Frey on* Larry King Live

My front four teeth are gone, I have a hole in my
cheek, my nose is broken and my eyes are swollen
nearly shut.
> —*James Frey, from* A Million Little Pieces

But I was there, 12C, window seat, and there
was no blood anywhere except the blue kind
making blue roots under the skin of our wrists.
From what I recall his teeth were all present,
ivory and symmetrical, one pristine incisor
flushed against the next like marble tiles.
Teeth other teeth aspire to be. I saw no hole
in his cheek but a razor nick or new pimple,
some red blip on his otherwise unblemished face.
Boyish. Babyish, even. The only holes
were the two he breathed from and the one
called a mouth that demanded another pillow,
headphones, club soda, more ice.
His nose was intact, straight as the tailfin
dividing the sky behind us. There was turbulence,
the plane a dragonfly in a windstorm.
My cup of Cabernet sloshed, my napkin bled,
a bag rumbled in the overheard bin like a fist
pounding inside a coffin. I was calm, I fly
all the time, but the man in question
was quivering and paler than a hardboiled egg.
Eyes swollen open, eyes skittering and green.
Or brown or blue. Memory is a murky thing,
always changing its mind. Interview me again
in three weeks and maybe I'll remember
his wounds, the way my grandmother
gradually put down the knife after she spread
butter on her napkin. Slowly the disease worked,
slowly erasing slowly what her brain slowly
recorded over the slowly decades. Memory
is a mysterious thing, shadow of a ghost,

nebulous as the clouds we pierced on our descent,
Chicago revealing itself in my little window
like dust blown from a photo of someone
it takes you a moment to recognize.

John Paul O'Connor

BEANS

The way my father told the story, it wasn't Jack who climbed
the Beanstalk. It was my sister and I. We were very,

very poor and my mother asked us to go sell the cow, whose part
my father gave to our dog, Igor. How sad I felt for my mother,

who was so desperate as to send her two young children
out into the world to bring home food for the family. Was this

why I discovered her one afternoon in her bedroom, sheer
white curtains feeding light onto her face as she wept? When we

came home with only beans to show for the cow we sold (what else
could we get for a cow that resembled a black Labrador?)

she screamed hysterically and sent us to our rooms without supper,
throwing the beans out the back door with a disillusionment

that was always with her. The narrator hid from the picture, omniscient
and absent, spending his time at the AmVet hall or at Nick's Tavern

where he learned the art of long elaborate tales which he told only
on the occasional nights when he drank at home and we gathered

around curious to know who he was. If he were sober he stayed
behind his newspaper and called for his supper like the giant

at the top of the beanstalk, growling at his tiny wife. Had he enough
to drink, the story would continue and the giant became

what we always hoped he would; a kind soul who did good work
for the people of the kingdom. But this wasn't a kingdom.

It was a four-bedroom house in Albuquerque in 1958 when there were
no giants, but plenty of dogs and children and drunken fathers

whose wives wept in the privacy of their afternoons and yelled
for their children at supper time. Food was on each table

and from my window I traced the long trunk of a poplar tree
to its top, where white flimsy clouds couldn't hold a thing.

Howard Price

CROW-MAGNON

Everybody's dying this week,
and for no good reason, that is, no money in it,
and suddenly second opinions are like men wearing
tiaras and women at the gym 4 days a week building huge
arms so they can both look better in a dress. For sure,
third and fourth opinions at a minimum now, since it occurs
to us that the real money's not in dying but living, and doing
whatever, to hide the forty years of duct tape that holds
us together, is not such an unreasonable ploy. The new plan is to
benefit the whole time we're alive, make out like undertakers,
even as we prolong the agony of playing second banana
to our bodies, as if playing second fiddle is too respectable,
as if the timbered glow of maple, spruce and willow
played by horsehair on sheep guts, is. It's impossible to stop
people from watching a crow and its chosen profession
of turning a wrapper over and over in the street for an hour
until it's found whatever isn't inside wasn't worth the effort.
Crows live in neither one of two moments of contemplation.
The transparent thoughts of their starless lifetimes
have yet to cross the endless reach of their one contiguous mind,
and before we count every step we've never taken back to home,
they'll pull each day from our thinning hair as needed,
while we watch amused, happy we're not so stupid.
Very often one crow gets what another crow wants.
Same goes for people. God can't tell us apart either.
Just watching the trick, the magic,
the reveal of how many ways the same thing
may be done to great or little effect, we, who are
so easily drawn to any mindless exhibition, end up
postponing strategies that could cure or move the world.
After a while, if we've lost our way and have deferred
the objective that we'd promised to commit to fully
for a crow's age, and another crow's age, and another
and another, we turn around and paste the blame
on the odd habits of a clever bird with fifty billion twins
that seems so happy unearthing a useless treasure
from a paper bag, and then shamefully admit
that watching its never-ending gig
is no less interesting to us, the very same,
who threw the bag on the street,
in the first place.

Patricia Smith

BIRTHDAY

On this bed of chilled steel, I am the morning's work,
your project after coffee and, oh yes, some woman's son.
Whistling to break the ice in the room, you hold
most of my head in your hands. Your shaping fingers
gently adjust an ear, probe a hollow eye socket,
flick chips of dried blood away from a blown-open
hairline. No one but you and I hear as you inhale
and, without exhaling, whisper the name I once had.

Grimacing, edging slowly toward overwhelm,
you clutch the photo, glancing from the grinning grad
to the exploded boy. Now the only sound in the room
is the flat hiss of the blade as you whittle a dim smile,
free fluid from my blue mouth. You reach into your bag
and pull out a nose, a sliver of chin, a ragged scalp,
and see them as just that—a shard of skin, that scalp.
You touch with the stark slowness of a lover, but you
don't cry out from that lover's deep bone. Just how
did you die your soul enough to be this temporary god,
stitching conjured light into the cave of my chest?

My mother sat across from you, tangled her hands
and re-scripted my days, wailing that the bullet
was meant for someone else, not me, not me, no,
not me, and *would you please make him the way he was,*
as close as you can to not dead, not dead, not gone,
and you said *yes.* You promised she'd be able to gaze
upon me and say, with that liquid hope in her voice,
He looks like he's sleeping. She's the reason you carve
and paste and snip with such focus, why you snap
my bones only to reset them, why you drag a comb
through the

I can't hear her voice anymore.
I can't hear the bullet slicing the night toward me.
I can't hear anything now but you,
whistling your perk past numb ritual,
stopping now and again to behold your gift
to the woman who first told you my name,
just before she handed you a picture
and begged you please, as best you can, *My baby.*

Alison Townsend

THE ONLY SURVIVING RECORDING
OF VIRGINIA WOOLF'S VOICE

I'm not expecting to hear her speak, stopped as I am
at a red light in Stoughton, Wisconsin, on the daily, desperate
dash home from work, my fractured spine throbbing
as if it housed my heart not my nerves, this snippet
on NPR as unexpected as recent November warm weather.
But here she is, sounding husky and a bit tired, her plummy
accent drawn out as she speaks about *words, English*
words...full of echoes and memories, associations
she does not name. It's still 1937 in her mouth
and later I'll learn that she's not really talking at all,
but reading a talk called "Craftsmanship" on the BBC's
program *Words Fail Me*, the script held up before her,
like a tablet of light in her long, white hands. Or a window
the sound of her voice opens in my head, her deliberate
phrasing a kind of eulogy to words and the way
They've been out and about on people's lips, in houses,
on the streets for so many centuries, time passing in the hiss
and skritch of the tape. As I imagine her in the studio,
a bit tense perhaps, her hair in that dark knot, dressed up,
though no one will see her, though years later her nephew
will describe the recording as too fast, too flat, barely
recognizable, her beautiful voice (though not so beautiful
as Vanessa's, he'll add) deprived of all resonance and depth.
But I don't know this as I listen, nothing to compare her to
but the sound her words made in my American head, as I lay
on my narrow dorm bed in my first November in college,
underlining phrase after phrase from *To the Lighthouse*
in turquoise or fuchsia ink, not because I understood
what they meant but because they sounded beautiful
aloud and my teacher had her photograph up in her office.
After my mother died, the first thing I forgot was the sound
of her voice, nothing to preserve it but a moment or two
on tape where she speaks in the background, saying
"Not now, not now," as if no time would ever be right, even
that scrap vanished somewhere in the past. Though I recall it
as I listen to Virginia Woolf, her voice—which is nothing
like my mother's, which my Woolf-scholar friend tells me
she "needs some time to get used to"—drifting on for eight
entire minutes, a kind of dream one could fall into, *as words*
stored with other meaning, other memories spill like smoke

from her throat and the light changes, and I drive on
through the gathering darkness, thinking about voices
and where they go when we die, how to describe pain
then leave it behind, her *lamp in the spine*
glowing, briefly lighting my way.

Emily Kagan Trenchard

THIS IS THE PART OF THE STORY
I'D RATHER NOT TELL

how at 13 I would lay awake at night deciding
which friend or family member would have to die
so that I might be aggrieved enough to be interesting,
so that I would have the permission to become more
withdrawn and mysterious and thus, more attractive.
I'd lay awake at night, plotting who it should be, how
it should go for the maximum impact. It would have
to be something epic so that I could become a rag doll
in his arms, bury my sweet face in the meaty expanse
of his 13-year-old chest and breathe deep the scent of his
Old Spice for my consolation. My malaise would surely
cause me to lose my appetite, and thus the tragic death
of my loved one would conveniently double as a diet plan.
In the version of the story where a masked gunman
breaks into our school and holds us all hostage, I am
always able to tackle him after he gets off a few
shots. One of them hits me non-fatally in the shoulder
and my current infatuation takes off his shirt to help
staunch the bleeding. I'm not sure how the story proceeds
from there because at this point in my dream I always
began to masturbate. I had determined that certain aunts
and cousins were important, but ultimately non-essential
enough to my daily life to be suitable options. Certain friends
had also been earmarked as acceptable, and I would update
my list with god each evening, playing through the
circumstances of their death and grieving each one with
actual tears so god might see what good choices I had made.
I didn't want him to think I had cheaped out and picked a
distant relative or a secret enemy to exchange for my love's
fulfillment. What kind of love would that be, anyway?

When it finally happened, there was no one but the floor
to fall into. Nothing but the gasping choke for my consolation.
I wouldn't let anyone touch me. The sacrificial loved one?
My best friend with the crooked smile and first kiss around
the corner, her mother who kissed my head like a daughter,
her father who would fetch me midnight bowls of cereal,
her sister, getting ready to start college. The epic disaster?
An exploding plane.
To whom much is given, much is expected.
I no longer speak to god.
I love like I'd kill for it.

TRIBUTE TO THE SONNET

ARTWORK BY STACIE PRIMEAUX

ARTWORK

Cover/Divider: *Ageless*, acrylic on canvas, 18" x 24"

STACIE PRIMEAUX lives in Austin, TX with her two beautiful children and a bunny. She works in a flower shop, and enjoys swimming, painting, photography, writing and reading. Her poem "Relic" appeared in *RATTLE* #25, and was runner-up for the first annual Neil Postman Award for Metaphor. Prints of her paintings, including *Ageless*, can be purchased online at the following address.

www.redbubble.com/people/concretekissed

T. S. Davis

THE RECRUDESCENCE OF THE MUSE: ONE POET'S JOURNEY

Freedom is only truly freedom when it appears against the background of an artificial limitation.
—T. S. Eliot

Rhythm and rhyme. Rhythm and rhyme. Rhythm and muthafucking rhyme.
—George Clinton

I went through graduate school in poetry under the workshop paradigm that came to dominance in the 1960s as a result of professors who had rejected formal verse for free verse in their own writing. The thinking was that there was no need to teach the outdated metrical rules, forms, and techniques of traditional poetry because rhyme and meter had been replaced universally by free verse. In many cases, this resulted in an abdication of teaching altogether and the professor became simply a workshop facilitator for the many student voices who critiqued each other's work. This was a qualitative change in the study of prosody which is the study of rhythm, rhyme, meter, stress, and language in poetry. For the first time, poets were being trained to be poets without being taught the traditional techniques of writing poetry. I could understand the teaching of the techniques of free verse in place of rhyme and meter, but free verse prosody itself seemed to be in its exuberant infancy, and still not well defined, despite 100 years of Whitman's progeny. So no system of versification, whether traditional or modern, was taught. The only prosody I learned was that of my fellow graduate students as we sat around and talked about our poems and how to write them. For two decades afterwards, by default, I wrote free verse poetry pretty much exclusively.

Except that I also wrote songs and was the singer for several rock bands. As I brought my poetry skills to bear on my lyrics, the use of meter and rhyme in my songs began to influence my poetry. Soon, even without music, I found myself counting measures and stresses and enjoying a newfound strength in the implosive power of a more formal prosodic structure. The line between my poems and songs began to blur as more frequently I took poems and adapted them to rhyming lyrics.

I remember looking at one of my older poems one day. It had been written back in the graduate school workshop almost twenty years before. Out of habit, I scanned the unrhymed lines to determine the rhythm pattern. To my surprise and revelation, I had written a perfect iambic pentameter blank verse poem at a time when I prided myself as a rebel against convention. Iambic pentameter is a line of ten syllables with the rhythmic stress on every other syllable, for a total of five stresses or beats per line.

Although there are many other rhythm patterns, iambic pentameter poetry constitutes the overwhelming majority of all English poetry written prior to the twentieth century. The fact that I could unconsciously but flawlessly write an entire poem using that rhythm made me think that somehow it was not just an artificial construction but one of the natural and fundamental rhythms of the English language, maybe even its heartbeat. Yet as a poet, I was ignorant of how to consciously manipulate it, or any of the other accoutrements of traditional prosody, to my own ends. At that moment, I knew this had to change if I were to grow as a poet. I could not afford to ignore what had been so painstakingly learned and perfected by generations of poets before me. To figure out where poetry was going, I felt I had to know where it was coming from. Or as Eliot put it, "There is no escape from metre; there is only mastery."

That was the day I started teaching myself the prosody that had its antecedents in old Anglo-Saxon—the language modern English grew out of— the prosody that was born in Chaucer, and then refined through Shakespeare, Pope, Keats, and countless others. I realized I had accepted the benefits of the new without bothering to learn the lessons of the old.

At the same time, in the late 1980s, I was also beginning to listen to hip hop under the influence of my young nephew, who was still in high school, and had made it his goal to open his old rocker uncle's ears to the new sound by sending tape after tape of his favorite groups. I was often amazed. Present were many of the elements of free verse prosody wedded to heavily cadenced rhyme: vocal presence or persona, wordplay, the specificity of vocabulary first engineered by Whitman, speed and breath control, the most personal of details jumbled with broad political swipes, braggadocio and humor, repetition and litany, all tied together with heavy meter and rhyme.

I started scanning the lyric sheets from Public Enemy and other groups. There were lots of metrically irregular lines, but iambic pentameter and tetrameter (four beats per line) tended to predominate. The traditional metrical "rules" were broken wide open, such as the prohibition against rhyming unstressed or weak syllables. In fact, what was considered frivolous and even clownish in traditional rhyming was the mark of highest skill in hip hop—the rhyming of words with multiple syllables or all the syllables of a multi-syllabic word being rhymed with a run of shorter words. Several slant or off rhymes could be used to "evolve" a rhyme into a completely different rhyming sound in the course of several lines. Enunciation could be exaggerated to make assonant and consonant rhymes prominent. These last two skills are what make Eminem such an amazing rapper, for instance. Traditional prosody tries to hide end rhyme with enjambment, making sure the sentence does not end with a rhyming word at the end of a line, but instead wraps into the next line. This hides the sound of the end rhyme in the middle of the sentence. But in hip hop prosody, the rhyme is proudly emphasized. In fact, overwhelming the listener with a plethora of rhyming sounds is much of the point in hip hop.

How ironic that as free verse prevailed from mid-century onward, it took a group of artists from outside the academy, way outside, from America's black ghettoes, to revolutionize poetic prosody irrevocably, despite their lack of acknowledgement from the academy even today. I think the academy preferred to set up the more pedantic of the New Formalists as a less dangerous paper tiger to argue against. At least the New Formalists flattered the academy by desiring recognition from it. But doctrinaire fascination with traditional technique, combined with contempt for Modernism, made the New Formalists an easier target to be labeled reactionary, thus discrediting their return to form.

So the true innovators in the resurgence of formalism were the rappers who embraced the power of rhythm and rhyme but radically transformed both to meet the needs of their content, breaking and making rules as they went. Being outside the academy, the full impact of their influence has yet to be felt. But it eventually will be, in the same way, for instance, that Bob Dylan and John Lennon tangentially influenced an earlier generation of poets. The impact has already been fully felt among younger poets, slam poets, and performance poets in general who eagerly use the full toolbox of techniques available to them including meter and rhyme. One prominent example of this new type of poet who commands respect in hip hop *and* academic circles is Saul Williams.

Ironically, some in the academy complain that this formalism among rappers and young performance poets has occurred without conscious awareness or appreciation of traditional English prosody. They may have a point. But they can't have it both ways. As guardians of the canon, they hid the keys to the toolbox and then complained that the keys were stolen.

T. S. Eliot himself had predicted that the free verse experiments of Modernism would eventually lead poets back to formalism. He saw the deviation from traditional prosody as a necessary corrective, as a "contrast between fixity and flux, this unperceived evasion of monotony, which is the very life of verse." Presumably, the same fate of monotony would eventually befall free verse itself without an infusion of formalism for contrast. Eliot explains himself best in his essay "Reflections on Vers Libre" from which the quotes above are taken. But he demonstrates his concept of contrasting fixity with flux most demonstrably in "The Love Song of J. Alfred Prufrock."

A couple of years ago, I was asked back to my undergraduate alma mater for a poetry reading and to sit in on a class taught by my old mentor, the poet Ron Bayes. Ron is an excellent teacher. He is a Modernist, an Imagist, a Pound scholar, and completely eclectic in his aesthetic tastes. What little I knew about formalism before graduate school I had learned from him as an undergraduate when he had made me write in all the major forms, much to my grumbling and dislike at the time.

The class was discussing "Prufrock" that day and I was expected to provide them with some insight into the master. I had dusted off my slim volume of Eliot in preparation and reread the poem for the hundredth time. But since the last time I had read it, I had written about 75 Shakespearian sonnets. A sonnet is typically a fourteen line poem of iambic pentameter meter with a strict end rhyming pattern. The type of sonnet written by Shakespeare always ends with a rhyming couplet. So my eye was trained to take in fourteen lines at a gulp. My mouth dropped open as I read the first stanza, composed of twelve lines, followed by a space, and then the famous rhyming couplet, "In the room the women come and go/ Talking of Michelangelo," for a total of fourteen lines.

This was something I had read many times, but never really recognized for what it is. Eliot opened "Prufrock" with an embedded sonnet! Can this really be, I thought? I scanned ahead. The next time the famous couplet appears in the poem, it's also preceded by a discrete stanza of twelve lines. Quickly I looked back to the beginning sequence to scan the meter. Four beats, five beats, six beats, three beats per line, and so on, irregular regularity, the way some heartbeats are classified. Taking into account slant rhyme and off rhyme, I scanned the sonnets this way. The first I artificially broke into lines of three, tercets, to make the rhyme structure more obvious: AAB CCB BDD EFF GG. For the second I used the traditional quatrain, lines of four, to the same purpose: ABCA BDCD EFFE GG. From these scansions, it was clear to me that Eliot fully knew what he was doing. Continuing to read through, I found other remnants of form, pieces of potential sonnets, but never again complete fourteen line poems.

I pointed all this out to the class, using a chalk board to demonstrate, letting them sound out the beats and rhymes. It seemed to be a revelation to them as well. I suggested that this poem was the object lesson of the place Eliot occupied in poetry. He relied heavily on forms, but shattered them for contrast, for fluidity, for the sake of the poem rising out of the ruins of what had gone before. I suggested the class look at the poem structurally as a tightly controlled explosion of form to counter the prevailing view that Eliot wrote outside of form, or formlessly. I suggested his work echoed the cubism of Picasso, built upon and growing out of the representation that preceded it, but deconstructing it, taking it apart and exposing its architecture to suggest that what we take for granted as natural is really just the bias of familiarity. The poem demonstrated Eliot's point in its transmogrification of the old into the new. Eliot knew the old rules. But he had the street cred and the balls to break them.

Eliot's concept is not that far from Robert Frost's notion: "Work easy in harness."

When I started my self-study of traditional English prosody, I set myself the task of learning the old rules, the old forms, with the clear intention of using what I learned to push my own poetry into the future, to build on the prosody of the canon, including the prosody of free verse incidentally, but to "Make it new," in the words of Ezra Pound. What I did not anticipate, but probably should have, was that the form would also make me new.

In my own writing, primarily Shakespearian sonnets now, I often deviate from the traditional metrical rules of accentual syllabic poetry by using a looser and freer scansion that conforms to my own idiosyncratic modern ear. Instead of parsing each arcane type of metrical unit (and practically every rhythmic deviation from iambic pentameter has a name), I count the overall beats in the line in much the same way it was done in Old English or Anglo-Saxon, the predecessor to Modern English. In my prosody, any number of unstressed syllables can be glossed over because what really matters is that strong thumping beat, similar to the sprung rhythm of Gerard Manley Hopkins. And like Geoffrey Chaucer, who basically "invented" iambic pentameter by combining the heavily stressed beats of Anglo Saxon with the syllabic poetry of his day, I have no prohibition on using a four beat or six beat line as needed. In fact, I often use the hexameter or Alexandrine couplet (six beats per line) for the final rhyming couplet of a sonnet. If the Alexandrine line divides naturally into two tercets, I find that the rhythm signals a distinctive counterpoint to the preceding pentameter. It slows down the reading and creates a visceral change in emotional content.

My cobbled aesthetic creates its own acceptance problems when I submit my poems for publication. On the one hand, I've received letters from editors who heartily objected to my formalism. On the other hand, I've received letters from editors who heartily objected to my cavalier notions of scansion when all my lines were not perfect iambic pentameter. I've found my work is often considered too formal for the free verse mags, too ragged for the formal mags. But what I find particularly comical are some of the descriptions of what an editor is looking for in *Poet's Market*. Often an editor will say that if a submission is rhymed, it must be of the "highest quality," whereas no such demand is enjoined on free verse. Apparently mediocre free verse submissions are less suspect and welcomed. Editors also ask that no "greeting card verse" be submitted, but apparently no restrictions apply to unrhymed free verse doggerel.

When I was a young man, I was much more confident about my ideas of the world and the impact I intended to have on the world. I had no doubt that my art, obscure as it was at the time, would one day take its place in the great canon of literature. I had all the time in the world to make it so. But now, at the age of sixty, I no longer have that time, and I certainly haven't received the level of accolade that as a young man I had anticipated would automatically follow the recognition of what I naively thought was my undeniable talent. It has not helped me, of course, to buck the dominant academic paradigm of free verse with my turn to an invented formalism in late career. I look back wistfully, not so much with regrets, as with the desire to be able to talk to that young man, to tell him some things I have learned about the nature of life, and of poetry.

But looking back, I also realize I didn't have much to say then in my poetry that wasn't just an extension of my fairly rigid ideology. The older I got the less confident I was and the more I understood how little I knew about the world and how little my work is likely to influence the world. Paradoxically, now I seem to have more to say and I'm a better writer than I've ever been, though less well known than I once was. Somehow one needs to know less to know more.

I often think about the story of Antonin Artaud. He sent some poems to an editor who basically told him they sucked. Artaud struck up a correspondence with him, vehemently defending and explaining in prose pieces his rejected poems. The editor replied that the poems still sucked but that his defense of them—full of angst and passion and paradox—was brilliant, and he wanted permission to publish it. Those pieces became the prose poetry for which Artaud is most revered today. And his rejected poems still suck!

What this says to me is that beneath the assertion, is the real question.

I toyed with rhyme and meter for years, working it into my poems, creating new forms of my own fancy. And then one day in 2002, under the influence of a cobalt blue Arizona sky, alcohol, and John Keats, I took a leap and started writing Shakespearian sonnets, one after the other, exclusively. The first ones were like a child's finger-painting, full of spirit, but naïve, as I was somewhat ignorant of what I had undertaken. But the sonnets came one after another, usually one a week, for months, and I was exhilarated. After a couple dozen, I thought if Shakespeare could write 154 of these suckers, then I can write 155! And so I set myself the juvenile task of doing just that. As stupid as that may sound, it has often been a motivator for me when nothing else was. I just recently broke through 100 sonnets, some good, some bad, but I continue to write them. But the better I get at writing sonnets, which is another way of saying the better I become at understanding the form of the sonnet, the harder they become to write, and the longer they take.

From the beginning what really surprised me was this: I didn't know where they were coming from.

When I started writing poetry over 40 years ago, I wrote all free verse. I was making up all the rules then under the influence of the Modernists, deciding the shape or shapelessness of each poem according to what I needed to express myself, yet much of what I wrote then tended to sound the same. My content determined my form. And there is a point of view that says that is as it should be, that form should serve content.

But now, 40 years later, I come to the same template for each poem— fourteen lines of iambic pentameter with a rigid rhyme scheme—yet I am continually amazed at how different each sonnet can end up sounding, at how this form can put the poetry under such intense pressure and yield such different results.

I'm also amazed at what I end up saying because usually I'm six to eight lines into the sonnet before I know what the poem is actually about, such are the hidden alleyways that rhyme and form lead you through. Toi Derricotte, in an interview in *Rattle*, once said, "I think a lot of times poems know things that we're not ready to know yet, and we write the poem and then we figure it out."

And even when I do know, I never know how it will end until it just does, because the rhyme controls where it goes. And that's really odd because there is no stronger nor assertive couplet in English prosody than lines thirteen and fourteen of a Shakespearian sonnet. How could one start a sonnet not knowing where it's going but knowing that twelve lines later a lyrical certainty, an epigram of unimpeachable elegance, would be required?

What this says to me is that beneath the question, is the real assertion.

It also says that my form determines my content.

Or maybe something else does, masquerading as form.

At the risk of waxing mystical, I must admit that writing sonnets has rejuvenated my belief in what the ancients called the Muse. Sonnets can be incredibly labor intensive and agonizing to write. So "finding" my way through the maze that the form creates, eliminating one rhyming dead end after another yet eventually coming out the other end, all gives me the strong intuitive feeling that I have been guided, led, coaxed into places I would not normally go by the "form" and made to discover what seems to have already and always existed. The more well wrought the sonnet, the more organic it feels, the harder it is to imagine a time when it did not exist.

This is a shock for a long time materialist such as myself. I do not pretend to understand it. I often feel like a translator of an ancient language no one else speaks with an incumbency to ensure the received wisdom is meticulously transcribed and correct. I never really felt that way writing free verse. Writing free verse, I often felt the exhilaration of what Kerouac called "spontaneous composition" when a free verse piece seemed to burst forth from nowhere completed on first writing with little or no editing needed. But I never felt the deep laborious ache that resolves so beautifully at the end of writing a good sonnet.

I have learned a few things about Shakespearian sonnets, commensurate with my modest chops. I usually start with a line I really like. Since I usually don't know what I'm doing, I might as well start with something I like. There is absolute freedom in that first line, in fact, in the first two lines. But after that, the direction is dictated by the rhyme. If you're used to writing free verse, this will come as a shock to you. You will need to learn to follow, not lead, or you will quickly find yourself down a rhymeless dead end, a babbling cul de sac, and have to hit the backspace key over and over until you've eaten that first line or two you loved and you're staring at blank paper again. That's when what you thought this sonnet was about crumbles and you realize George Clinton nailed it: "Rhythm and rhyme. Rhythm and rhyme. Rhythm and muthafucking rhyme." At that point you have a choice to make: quit, or trust the form to show you where to go.

Years ago, when I told a poet friend I was writing sonnets, he said that he assumed I was writing a free verse poem first and then manipulating it to make the shoe fit. I just laughed at the fanciful notion that I could impose the sonnet onto a poem. No, instead, the sonnet allows entrance—what you do inside determines whether you're worthy of the form. It doesn't conform to you; you conform to it.

But even with the form pulling you in the direction of a particular rhyming sound, the choices of where you can go in the labyrinth of the sonnet are still pretty much inexhaustible. Yet like the I Ching, the wisdom a sonnet can reveal as you write it is often serendipitous.

You may choose to bleed a sentence from the first quatrain into the second quatrain at line five in a Shakespearian sonnet, and that's okay, but unless you wish to drive yourself crazy, truly crazy, trust me, put a period at the end of line eight. The first eight lines set up the problem. Line nine is "the turn," and like "the river" in poker, fortunes should change, possibilities appear, or more in keeping with the extended metaphor, you should feel the centrifugal force of going too fast around a hairpin curve. So like Shakespeare himself, start line nine with a nice qualifier, such as *but*, or *yet*, or at least start a new sentence to signal your reader that change is coming.

You've now only got four lines to solve your dilemma. By now, the sonnet should have revealed to you what it's about, what problem you are trying to resolve. Only four lines are left to basically end the poem, the first time, that is. Most sonnets have an organicity, a degree of resolution, by the end of line twelve. But it ain't over yet: the biggest challenge of any Shakespearian sonnet is the final rhyming couplet.

The word sonnet in Italian means "little song." And it is that, but "little" is also deceptive. A sonnet is little in the way a firecracker is little or in the way a toddler squalling his heart out on the floor is little. I think of the sonnet as a pattern of energy tightly pressurized and shaped by the tight constraints of the form. Eliot's injunction of an "artificial limitation" is relevant again. At the risk of sounding ludicrous, I compare a sonnet to the internal combustion engine. Gasoline will always burn, but if you add a spark to a mixture of gasoline and air inside a cylinder, the resulting *explosion* is shaped by the cylinder and directed toward the end where a piston moves. It is the constraint of energy that creates the power. In a sonnet, that constrained energy is directed toward the final rhyming couplet, and the power, the tension, is released there. The couplet is no denouement. It is a full on climax, in every nuance of the word.

The final rhyming couplet is why I write Shakespearian sonnets instead of Petrarchan sonnets. Those two lines can be some of the most powerful and elegant lines in English poetry. They definitely end the sonnet on a much higher level of meaning than line twelve, while often standing alone at the same time as though a rarefied form of English haiku: "In the room the women come and go/ Talking of Michelangelo."

A sonnet needs its couplet, but a couplet can often lead its own life. Any of us would be proud to be included in the canon for a body of work, for a book, or for a single poem. I would settle for a single rhyming couplet, cut off from its sonnet and author, anonymous and unattributed, quoted by unknown speakers at funerals, weddings, toasts, in bars, or in moments of triumph or despair. Is there any higher calling than to put your words on the tongue of the world? That is what the couplet should strive for, that is what anyone as a writer of sonnets should live for.

Unless of course...the couplet is crap. My best critic is Sue, my partner of twenty-five years. I cannot tell you the number of times I've thought I was done with a new sonnet, exhilarated that I had stumbled through it gracefully somehow without it all falling apart, and allowing myself to rise after hours of rearranging approximately 125 odd words to read it aloud to her, only to have her say something like: "You know I really like it—up until the last two lines. Somehow they feel a little weak to me. You need to rework them."

Dejected, intoxicated with rhyme, I'd return to my desk and try once more to fashion two elegant lines, for hours if need be. I try not to stop until I'm done—I don't dare risk the loss of momentum because I already have too many twelve line sonnets in want of one good couplet sitting stranded and helpless in a digital doc. And if I feel the Muse is listening, real or imagined, you can bet I will continue to quietly sing my "little song," to whisper my rhymes into the ear of the Muse. I also know that if it comes too easily, somehow it's not earned. When a breakthrough finally arrives, from somewhere, nowhere, often simple, or obvious, or understated, no matter how tired I am, and sonnets are exceedingly laborious, I feel elated, relieved, awed, overwhelmed, and most interestingly, grateful, not for something I've *done*, but for something I've *discovered*. Any pride I may feel is on behalf of the beauty of the sonnet itself.

As a young man I tried to show the world something that I thought was coming from me. Now I try to show the world something I have found. It can be argued that literary vision is different for the young than for the old. The young choose their ideas and try to change the world with them. And that is good. The old allow the world to change their ideas. And that is good.

Yet I would argue that the path one takes is continuous. The choices you make today are the basis for whom you will become tomorrow. Just as the person you were as a child is still within you, so the person you have not yet become exists within you as well. Just as the person you are today has answers to the questions you asked when you were young, the person you have not yet become has answers to the questions you are asking today. So a conversation with your past and your future is entirely appropriate, necessary, and for poets, that conversation occurs in poetry.

But I do not mean to suggest the way to Nirvana is to ensconce yourself in traditional forms like the sonnet. After all, you are who you are, so "Come as you are," in the words of Kurt Cobain. In fact, your view of the world and your character may lead you to destroy old forms and invent new ones in the same way Whitman used free verse as an axe to splinter nineteenth century prosody. If the Muse is poetry idealized, then as times change, so must the ideal—the Muse always demands the new. As poets we all need to be cognizant that the new tradition Whitman founded is still the dominant paradigm today and retains the faint aura of insurrection though it is now over 150 years old. No longer the revolution, free verse is now the status quo. And the Muse?—the Muse is bored, has been for a long time.

New art, whatever form it takes, can be brutal when it finally breaks free, suppressing what came before in order to gain dominance. But it also builds on top of what it obliterates. The Modernists ransacked the past for their influences, and they chose well: Greek literature, Japanese and Chinese poetry, the troubadours, Dante, the English Metaphysical poets, among others. What's important now is not *whom* they chose, but *that* they chose. Because that is the task that faces us. All poets before us have stood precisely at the crossroads we now face. We would be stupid to ignore their counsel. Without their work, however antiquated by current popular tastes, our own prosody would not exist. Any true formal revolution in poetry will be a step into the future, not the past. But it is the fixity of the past that distinguishes the flux of the future.

What transcends time and form is the ancient heartbeat of our Mother Tongue, old Anglo Saxon. It beats now strong, now faint, now regular, now irregular, but it beats still today in line after line of your poetry and mine. We can choose to palpate it, or not. But as Chaucer put it, "The lyfe so short, the craft so long to lerne."

T. S. DAVIS is the author of two books of poetry, *Sun + Moon Rendezvous* and *Criminal Thawts*. He lives in Asheville, NC. <redhawk27@charter.net>

Tony Barnstone

BAD USAGE

When in the mist of a phone call you loose
yourself in thought and all seams an allusion,
when I take you for granite like statues
of limitation, and the one solution
seams to excape like hoarses from a coral
fenced with Bob wire, than thoughts go wild, gallump-
ing off, and take a different tact. The morale
is when I spread whip cream on your volump-
tuous bawdy, when I gays at you awl rapt
up in duck tape of lust, its not enough.
We use each other viscously. We dangle
over a whole, unable to adept.
But cant we change? Lets nip it in the butt.
We kneed to see things from another angel.

Father and Daughter
by I.C. Rapoport

SILENCE TOOK MY TONGUE
WHEN MY BROTHER WENT

Silence took my tongue when my brother went
away, now words are skittery rabbits: soft,
furry lumps huddled in my throat's dry den.
I wait for him at breakfast where the clock
clicks its mean teeth, wait for him to tease me,
please Lord, anything, but his empty chair
staring back: a hard, narrow beast. Scary
to know one hundred sixteen children there
and then not. Scary the ambulances,
lights that would not end, turning the street blue.
Now I won't leave Father's side; who knows when
earth might tumble open, swallow him, too?
You know the queen flew here; kneeled down and prayed,
left a fancy white wreath on brother's grave.

NOTE ON THE SERIES FROM MICHELLE BITTING: "At the time I wrote
'Silence Took My Tongue...' and the other eleven sonnets in my
Aberfan series, I'd been admiring I.C. Rapoport's photography done
for *Life* magazine covering their 1966 disaster in Wales, when decades
of coal sludge slid down the mountain and covered a school full of
children, trapping them inside. My hope is that this collaborative
series combines to create documentation, elegy, and, ultimately, cele-
bration of survival and human existence, moving from grief to life-
affirmation."

Chris Bullard

BACK STORY

The mate in spandex straps us, front and back,
to flapping canvas sail and walks us back-
wards to the speedboat's slippery stern, back
to where the blue-green sea roils in the back-
wash. You shout, "This is great," but I shout back,
"Let's ask the captain for our money back."
And then a windstorm lifts us. Looking back,
I see us rising, slipping off the back
from safety into sky. The one way back
is down. I yell, "Too high!" and pull you back
though you're not scared—not here, or back
at home, where I press, sleeping, to your back,
afraid to lose you, who hold nothing back.

Wendy Taylor Carlisle

THE CIRCUS OF INCONSOLABLE LOSS

There is only one ring for those sweating horses with the preternaturally
flat backs and the fat smooth rumps from which ladies
in stained tights vault onto the sawdust
or another horse.

Only one ring for the hung-over clowns and their Volkswagen,
a car so old it must be pushed into the one ring
which is also the one for the acrobats and the tigers and contortionists
and dogs that walk on their hind legs,

then stop to scratch their necks, itchy under spangled ruffs. Above them
wire walkers and trapeze guys swing,
mayfly-graceful. Under them the one ring
reminds the audience to celebrate, each in their own

constrained and special way,
the emptiness they've come to in the spaces where other rings should be.

Peter Coghill

GABRIELLA

My little niece rakes leaves, then runs full tilt
into the pile, busting them up all over—
with joy and guilt, and joy sprung from that guilt,
she kicks and clouts about until they cover
the grass again. A two-year-old Godzilla
on the front lawn, reveling in a power
so new and physical. A last patch fills her
arms and she flings a red and golden shower—
of words. For that is how she talked as well,
with wonder at our comprehending her,
a welter, like the spray of leaves that fell
from her throw, and caught the sun as tongues of fire.
Inspiration on the shaggy wind
of autumn—soon to be swept up and binned.

T. S. Davis

WHOOPING RENDEZVOUS

Outside our bedroom window, we both heard
a whooping noise from somewhere in the dark,
and though an eerie call, it was a bird—
I'm sure of this—its cry forlorn and stark.
I looked outside across the midnight lawn.
Though nothing moved, yet I could feel it knew
that someone now was listening to its song,
deciphering this whooping rendezvous.
Of course, the whooping stopped—I knew it would—
and all returned to silent raw despair.
Yet we who heard have never understood
that tense and lonesome cry that split the air.
For every creature seeks to share its pain,
and then backs off, afraid to make it plain.

Paul Dickey

A KNACK FOR LOSING THINGS

The art of losing isn't hard to master.
—Elizabeth Bishop, "One Art"

What has been lost along my careless way
will not come back to me another day,
and let's be frank, it often will not do
to keep a useful thing its use past due.

Whether a love, or say, a fountain pen,
some things I have today, I won't again.
Please, if I lose a button, don't advise
because if I were then to realize,

I'd stop and stay behind too long to look
for what I should not find. The time it took
I could have used to buy a newer shirt,
not stoop to pick up what is claimed by dirt.

Every day a few things loved are lost.
To get them back comes at a greater cost.

BACKWARD SONNET
FOR A FORWARD THINKER

"If only I knew now what I'll know soon,"
he likes to say. His office is immune
to order, his lab the opposite. His team
built a molecular machine that walks
on strands of DNA. His childhood dream
was to become a poet. He gives talks
on nanosystems every fall—the hall
is packed. "Old forms must be replaced," he starts
(his intro doesn't change). "The past's a wall
between the present and future." Charts
and tables, fluctuating year to year,
support his points. He's photographed for *Time*.
He whispers to machines that can't (yet) hear:
turn right, turn left, step back, walk sideways, climb.

Jehanne Dubrow

The Cold War, A Romance

Sometimes we were illegal dollar bills.
We were the three-hour line for bread,
the last pair of pantyhose in the shop,
the hard potato. Or else, we were the town
of industry where all machines had stopped,
the stalled assembly line, the pneumatic drills.
We were the wiretap, the rumor spread
from room to room. We were the State crackdown.
And yes, we were the act of making do—
a soup of water, salt, a chicken bone.
We were the vodka swigged against the chill,
and the sad folk song that every soldier knew,
and the ribbon in the yellow hair, and the stone
that marked the fallen bodies on the hill.

DOVER

The cliff is white,
perpendicular to the sea,
covered with green
where the slope is kind.

I'm no farmer
but even I know
to not plant a seed
on up and down land.

So hold my hand
at the very edge
where safe becomes,
shall we say, slippery.

The cave is always near
where my monsters hide.

Carol Frith

BLACK TIGHTS, A HALTER TOP

She's waiting near the corner of Monroe
and Pierce: spike heels, black tights, a halter top,
her image coding sunlight. Who will stop,
eclipse this smolder that is burning slow
as incense on the walk? Is she a pro?
Perhaps, although a slowly cruising cop
on Pierce ignores her. Her cigarette's a prop.
She never takes a drag—a cameo
against the sun, her small face smiling at
whatever thing it is might fill her needs.
Two sparrows? The donut shop across the street?
At her back, an oak. The light is flat.
Pinned to the tree, a ragged sign that reads:
For sale. Persimmons, firm to the touch, and sweet.

COVER TO COVER

*Every passion borders on the chaotic, but the
collector's passion borders on the chaos of
memories.*
—Walter Benjamin

I don't collect them. They just accumulate,
Tower higher into shoddy columns,
Climbing weirdly like crystal formations
Or pillars of coral. The thought of their weight
Crushes, their long summers and snow. They weigh tons.
They slide onto the stove, under the fridge,
Into the tub. They prop open windows,
Serve as coasters. They have traveled with me
And slept beside me. They fashion a bridge
To vanished rooms, sorrows, and suns. Lord knows
Why I haul them from city to city.
I slip them together like bricks. They become a wall,
My greed, my fears, everything, nothing at all.

Luke Johnson

The Heart, Like a Bocce Ball

The jack sits low in the grass. We're dead drunk,
cannonballing across the lawn, gouging
handful divots, each of us still nursing
a tumbler of scotch brought home from the wake.
We sons and brothers and cousins. I spin
my ice and let that black-tie loosening
buzz swarm. The others choose the sky, looping
pop-flies that swirl with backspin, an earthen
thud answering grunts while the soft dirt caves.
I bowl instead, slow-ride hidden ridges—
the swells buried beneath the grass—carving
a curve, a line from start to stop, finish.
The heart, like a bocce ball, is fist-sized
and firm; ours clunk together, then divide.

Unholy Sonnet Number One

My bowl of lamb and gravy from the can
appears each morning when at last you rise.
An hour ago I batted at your eyes,
and it's been two since first the birds began.
My brother has already fouled the pan;
you slept right through his scratching and his cries
(their tone suggesting something oversize
and fetid, for which you'd require bran).
Your feet are on the floor. That's a relief.
Your awkward fingers soon will pop the lid
I yearn for, giving proof to my belief
that God made humans well the way He did.
You Big Ones, lacking claws and feline verve
were clearly planned to open cans—to serve.

Stephen Kessler

ANY HACK CAN CRANK OUT
A HUNDRED SONNETS

Any hack can crank out a hundred sonnets
if he has to; all you have to do
is set up your metronome and start typing,
taking dictation from the day's small gifts,
whatever presents itself in the street
or dredges itself up from memory
or dreams itself out of your transcribing hand.
It's an insidious form, because it's almost
easy, leading you by the wrist through rules
and rhythms as old as the English language
translated down the ages in idioms
transformed by time and driven by dying breaths.
It gives you a false sense of what you meant
when the closing couplet clinches your argument.

KNIVES OF THE POETS

The philosophers keep hammering, each
to each. Editors choose scissors. Critics
fancy the blunt: crowbars, mallets, and such.
Poets like knives. It starts at about six
in a fury of initials, hearts, and
arrows jack-knifed into the flesh of trees
(ash, sometimes; mostly elders). Understand
that aimless whittling comes next, and will lead
to the real work: Dr. Williams and his
scalpel, Anne Sexton's special set of trick
knives, complete with weighted hafts and circus
music, William Blake's cutlass, red and slick
as paint that paints demons. Parry, jab, thrust.
The world is our whetstone. We shall not rust.

Gregory Loselle

from THE WHOLE OF HIM COLLECTED

10

The box of papers on the closet floor
contains his discharge papers from the war,
a couple letters, dog tags: amulets
against prospective dangers, even bets
on futures filed away, here; telegrams
my grandmother amended in shorthand
notes ("*May God protect you*,") on their backs;
her death certificate, its seal (not wax
like his diplomas also here with hers)
stamped paper pressed into concentric curves
through pulp and print, disturbing the intent
of text accounting how her life was spent
a quarter century before—why keep
these things? For what? And why disturb their sleep?

LIBRARY LOVERS

She devours Steel, and he L'Amour.
She leads him to the fiction, where they part
for different shelves. He's eager to explore
the tough ol' west, and she the tough ol' heart.
They meet me at the desk with separate piles.
Unthinkingly, I mix the books together.
I sense his wave of nervousness. She smiles
and quickly sorts the titles out. "Nice weather
today," she says. He slides his pile away,
averts his eyes, and waits for her to pull
out bags. "Let's eat at Lou's," I hear her say.
She grabs his arm and leads him, tote bag full
of cowboy stories swinging at his heel,
his sidearm holstered by her whim of steel.

                    Make
                 Mine
              Darjeeling
                      by
                   Patti
                McCarty

It seems to me incredibly unfair
suggesting I get off my derrière
and poetize a picture. I don't care
to imitate your *Still Life With a Pear*;
it's not my cup of tea to write on   cue
for Carmen Figurewhat'shername or   you.
Reverse ekphrasis? I scorn those   who
can shape a song but cock-a-doodle-do
bereft of rhyme and meter's euphony
or manage to produce a chimpanzee
   by sacrificing line integrity;
      to pour words into shapes
            is gimmickry.
Such craft is rightly seen as mere pretension;
my poetry's the model of convention.

Mary Meriam

THE ROMANCE OF MIDDLE AGE

Now that I'm fifty, let me take my showers
at night, no light, eyes closed. And let me swim
in cover-ups. My skin's tattooed with hours
and days and decades, head to foot, and slim
is just a faded photograph. It's strange
how people look away who once would look.
I didn't know I'd undergo this change
and be the unseen cover of a book
whose plot, though swift, just keeps on getting thicker.
One reaches for the pleasures of the mind
and heart to counteract the loss of quicker
knowledge. One feels old urgencies unwind,
although I still pluck chin hairs with a tweezer,
in case I might attract another geezer.

Jessica Moll

COSTUME

Our game's a cross between *A Chorus Line*
and *Fame*. Rehearsals, here in our backyard.
Pretend the lawn's the stage. The tutu's mine,
but I let David pick a leotard.
I'm ten, he's five, he's used to all my rules.
He gets to be a girl, but has to choose
a neutral name like "Chris." Summer fog rolls
in. We swirl our glitter scarves to music
in our heads. He's got it down, the girl
pose: hips, hands. He's not a boy. He won't play
out front, racing Big Wheels. Instead, he twirls
barefoot with me. But what about the place
my fingers found, underneath my clothes?
The grass is cold. *Plié*. And point your toes.

AUBADE FOR ONE DISMAYED

Half-Alice in her milky, silky sheets
almost awake to the ache of another day
rebounding from her beaming ceiling,
grieved leaving the comforts of the night—
the snuggled pillow and the shy bedfellow
a fuzzy dream had borne and then withdrawn
at the intrusion of the hooligan light.

She closed her eyes once more to place the face,
so familiar and, yes, similar
to that of someone she had always known.
Perhaps she'd find a name if once again
she slipped into the deep warm sea of sleep.
And then a voice called Alice and she saw
a woman waving, craving her return.

PANOPHILIA

Love of everything

Today this weather's better than itself:
all background clamor, siren song, our schemed
and ill-conceiving strategies. This shelf,
chaotic and precariously leaning
next to your appalling bed, a trove
of wonders hovering over us. But love
itself I never deigned to love; all give
and giving in. So I don't understand
my drunkenness on scribble scrawled above
the mirror in the ladies' room: *You're doomed.*
Ecstatic that it's almost true. And though
I should not love you yet—obliged to slow
and genuflect to sense or self-defense—
because of you, I'll love everything else.

Catherine Esposito Prescott

TO A HURRICANE

At the right speed wind sounds like a train
        straining its breaks as metal grates metal;
but before you imagine sparks raining
        circles around the wheels, its voice changes
to a throaty hush. In the early stages, you may
        mistake it for the neighbors laughing, then crying.
As doors and windows tremble, as locks labor
        to stay closed, you'll hear the cry of the mother
burying her child by the river, and of widows
        who have lost everything to war. And in that moment
what remains of your sense of order is supplicant
        like the spine of a palm tree bowed toward earth, fronds beaten, torn,
and the sweet cord of belief that holds your life together
        fights like hell not to snap: the tree's trunk, your back.

Patricia Smith

MOTOWN CROWN

The Temps, all swerve and pivot, conjured schemes
that had us skipping school, made us forget
how mamas schooled us hard against the threat
of five-part harmony and sharkskin seams.
We spent our schooldays balanced on the beams
of moon we wished upon, the needled jet-
black 45s that spun and hadn't yet
become the dizzy spinning of our dreams.
Sugar Pie, Honey Bun, oh you
loved our nappy hair and rusty knees.
Marvin Gaye slowed down while we gave chase
and then he was our smokin' fine taboo.
We hungered for the anguished screech of *Please*
inside our chests—relentless, booming bass.

જી ભ્ઠ

Inside our chests, relentless booming bass
softened to the turn of Smokey's key.
His languid, liquid, luscious, aching plea
for bodies we didn't have yet made a case
for lying to ourselves. He could erase
our bowlegs, raging pimples, we could see
his croon inside our clothes, his pedigree
of milky flawless skin. Oh, we'd replace
our *daddies* with his fine and lanky frame,
I did you wrong, my heart went out to play
he serenaded, filling up the space
that separated Smoke from certain flame.
We couldn't see the drug of him—OK,
silk where his throat should be. He growled such grace.

Silk where his throat should be, and growling grace,
Little Stevie made us wonder why
we even *needed* sight. His rhythm eye
could see us click our hips and swerve in place
whenever *he* cut loose. Ooh, we'd unlace
our Converse All-Stars. Yeah, we wondered why
we couldn't get down *without* our shoes, we'd try
and dance and keep up with his funky pace
of hiss and howl and hum, and then he'd slow
to twist our hearts until he heard them crack,
ignoring what was leaking from the seams.
The rockin' blind boy couldn't help but show
us light. We bellowed every soulful track
from open window, 'neath the door—pipe dreams.

From open windows, 'neath the doors, pipe dreams
taught us bone, bouffant and nicotine
and served up Lady D, the boisterous queen
of overdone, her body built from beams
of awkward light. Her bug-eyed brash extremes
dizzied normal girls. The evergreen
machine, so clean and mean, dabbed kerosene
behind our ears and said *Now burn*. Our screams
meant only that our hips would now be thin,
that we'd hear symphonies, wouldn't hurry love,
as Diana said, *Make sure it gleams
no matter what it is*. Her different spin,
a voice like sugar air, no inkling of
a soul beneath the vinyl. The Supremes.

That soul beneath the vinyl, the Supremes
knew nothing of it. They were breathy sighs
and fluid hips, soul music's booby prize.
But Mary Wells, so drained of self-esteem,
was a pudgy, barstool-ridin' buck-toothed dream
who none of us would dare to idolize
out loud. She had our mamas' grunt and thighs
and we preferred to just avoid THAT theme—
as well as war and God and gov'ment cheese
and bullets in the street and ghetto blight.
While Mary's "My Guy" blared, we didn't think race,
'cause there was all that romance, and the keys
that Motown held. Unlocked, we'd soon ignite.
We stockpiled extra sequins, just in case.

We stockpiled extra sequins, just in case
the Marvelettes decided that our grit
was way beyond Diana's, that we fit
inside their swirl, a much more naughty place.
Those girls came from the brick, we had to brace
ourselves against their heat, much too legit
to dress up as some other thing. We split
our blue jeans trying to match their pace.
And soon our breasts commenced to pop, we spoke
in deeper tones, and Berry Gordy looked
and licked his lips. Our only saving grace?
The luscious, liquid languid tone of Smoke,
the soundtrack while our A-cup bras unhooked.
Our sudden Negro hips required more space.

೫ ଓଃ

Our sudden Negro hips required more space,
but we pretended not to feel that spill
that changed the way we walked. And yes, we still
couldn't help but feel so strangely out of place
while Motown filled our eager hearts with lace
and Valentines. Romance was all uphill,
no push, no prod, no shiny magic pill
could lift us to that light. No breathing space
in all that time. We grew like vines to sun,
and then we burned. As mamas shook their heads
and mourned our Delta names, we didn't deem
to care. Religion—there was only one.
We took transistor preachers to our beds
and Smokey sang a lyric dripping cream.

೫ ଓଃ

While Smokey sang a lyric dripping cream,
Levi tried to woo us with his growl:
Can't help myself. Admitted with a scowl,
his bit of weakness was a soulful scheme—
and we kept screaming, front row, under gleam
of lights, beside the speakers' blasting vowels,
we rocked and screamed. Levi, on the prowl,
glowed black, a savior in the stagelight's beam.
But then the stagelight dimmed, and there we were
in bodies primed—for what we didn't know.
We sang off-key while skipping home alone.
Deceptions that you sing to tend to blur
and disappear in dance, why is that so?
Ask any colored girl and she will moan.

Ask any colored girl and she will moan
an answer with a downbeat and a sleek
five-part croon. She's dazzled, and she'll shriek
what she's been taught: She won't long be alone,
or crazed with wanting more. One day she'll own
that quiet heart that Motown taught to speak,
she'll know that being the same makes her unique.
She'll rest her butt on music's paper throne
until the bassline booms, until some old
Temptation leers and says *I'll take you home
and heal you in the way the music vowed.*
She's trapped within his clutch, his perfumed hold,
dancing to his conjured, crafted poem,
remembering how. Love had lied so loud.

Remembering how love had lied so loud,
we tangled in the rhythms that we chose.
Seduced by thump and sequins, heaven knows
we tried to live our looming lives unbowed,
but bending led to break. We were so proud
to mirror every lyric. Radios
spit beg and mend, and precious stereos
told us what we were and weren't allowed.
Our daddies sweat in factories while we
found other daddies under limelight's glow.
And then we begged those daddies to create
us. Like Stevie, help us blindly see
the rhythms, but instead, the crippling blow.
We whimpered while the downbeat dangled bait.

We whimpered while the downbeat dangled bait,
we leapt and swallowed all the music said
while Smokey laughed and Marvin idly read
our minds and slapped us hard and slapped us straight,
and even then, we listened for the great
announcement of the drum, for tune to spread,
a Marvelette to pick up on the thread.
But as we know by now, it's much too late
to reconsider love, or claw our way
through all the glow they tossed to slow our roll.
What we know now we should have always known.
When Smokey winked at us and then said *They
don't love you like I do,* he snagged our soul.
We wound up doing the slow drag, all alone.

ဆ ၑ

They made us do the slow drag, all alone.
They made us kiss our mirrors, deal with heat,
our bodies sudden bumps. They danced deceit
and we did too, addicted to the drone
of revelation, all the notes they'd thrown
our way: *Oh, love will change your life. The sweet
sweet fairy tale we spin will certainly beat
the real thing any day. Oh, yes we own
you now. We sang you pliable and clue-
less, waiting, waiting, oh the dream you'll hug
one day, the boy who craves you right out loud
in front of everyone. But we told you,
we know we did, we preached it with a shrug—
less than perfect love was not allowed.*

Less than perfect love was not allowed.
Temptations begged as if their every sway
depended on you coming home to stay.
Diana whispered air, aloof and proud
to be the perfect girl beneath a shroud
of glitter and a fright she held at bay.
And Michael Jackson, flailing in the fray
of daddy love, succumbed to every crowd.
What would we have done if not for them,
wooing us with roses carved of sound
and hiding muck we're born to navigate?
Little did we know that they'd condemn
us to live so tethered to the ground.
While every song they sang told us to wait.

Every song they sang told us to wait
and wait we did, our gangly heartbeats stunned
and holding place. Already so outgunned
we little girls obeyed. And now it's late,
and CDs spinning only help deflate
us. The songs all say, *Just look what you've done,*
you've wished through your whole life. And one by one
your stupid sisters boogie to their fate.
So now, at fifty plus, I turn around
and see the glitter drifting in my wake
and mingling with the dirt. My dingy dreams
are shoved high on the shelf. They're wrapped and bound
so I can't see and contemplate the ache.
The Temps, all swirl and pivot, conjured schemes.

The Temps, all swirl and pivot, conjured schemes
inside our chests, relentless booming bass
then silk where throats should be. Much growling grace
from open window, 'neath the door, pipe dreams—
that soul beneath the vinyl. The Supremes
used to stockpile extra sequins just in case
Diana's Negro hips required more space,
while Smokey penned a lyric dripping cream.
Ask any colored girl, and she will moan,
remembering how love had lied so loud.
I whimpered while the downbeat dangled bait
and taught myself to slow drag, all alone.
Less than perfect love was not allowed
and every song they sang told me to wait.

Elizabeth Klise von Zerneck

FREEDOM
Haight Street

The realtor claimed the flat was lived in once
by Janis Joplin, a quite common claim,

we later learned. The tactic worked on us.
We learned to overlook—that hint of fame!—

the smell of gas, an awkward floor plan, soot
that never scoured. We dwelled not there but on

our plum address and, when fall came, we bought
dark Goodwill coats, the nights much colder than

we had foreseen. Through that long year, we read
Jacques Derrida, and smoked, and grew fresh thyme

on the one sill with light. We baked wheat bread—
well, one loaf anyway—and drank red wine,

and each day died a bit—twenty, confused—
two other words for nothing left to lose.

Thom Ward

RUMPUS, COHESION, MESS

The bed sheet knows the vices I've slept.
How quickly it nooses my feet. Someone said,
we're wrong men in a right world, all that
zigzag anger. Not quite—that's another movie.
We're wrong men who've built a wrong world,
each with a knapsack full of crushed glass,
cigarette butts. Photos of our children march
off the walls to a music only the dog can hear.
Rumpus minus cohesion equals mess. So many
weapons, I'm waiting for the plunger to make
the first move. Why should the water play fair.
Is that a cross around your neck or the last bird?
Things forgotten scream out for help in dreams
but not as loudly as things remembered.

Donald Mace Williams

THE VENTURI EFFECT

You may have thought, from visiting art shows,
that canyons squeezed together on their way
downstream. No. That's only perspective. They
in fact, as any hiker my age knows,
spread out and vanish. Their canyonness goes.
Their vital currents pool up, slacken, splay,
their tall red hoodoos melt into flat gray,
the bankside cottonwoods go, nothing grows.
This one the same. Far downstream now, my feet
have brought me where I see the end. No foam
from water straitened, focused one last time
by rock walls aping art, trying to meet,
but alkali-white flatlands, killdeers' home,
walls gone, speed gone, all low that was high prime.

John Yohe

THE GHOST OF FRANK O'HARA

The ghost of Frank O'Hara taps me on
the shoulder whispering
              and what about
the humor what about talks with the sun
and things that happen at the movies out
of sight of parents don't forget the thirst
of being in Manhattan in the heat
and Coke the drink
               remember too your first
love passion music though it might not come out
in words it's there in you but I was sad
and said what good is humor in a poem
when people die Manhattan Fire Island
we
    bought falafels which we thought weren't bad
and walked to Central Park for space and some
children were laughing and he said ask them

A Conversation with Alice Fulton

photo by Hank De Leo

ALICE FULTON is the author of eight books, including *The Nightingales of Troy: Connected Stories*; *Cascade Experiment: Selected Poems*; and an essay collection, *Feeling as a Foreign Language: The Good Strangeness of Poetry*. Among her honors are fellowships from the MacArthur Foundation, the National Endowment for the Arts, and The Bobbitt Prize for Poetry from the Library of Congress for her collection *Felt*. Her other poetry books include *Sensual Math*, *Powers of Congress*, *Palladium*, and *Dance Script With Electric Ballerina*. Fulton's poetry and fiction have been chosen repeatedly for *The Best American Poetry*, *The Best American Short Stories*, and Pushcart Prize anthologies. Currently the Ann S. Bowers Professor of English at Cornell, she also has taught at the University of Michigan, UC Berkeley, and UCLA.

Conversation Between Alice Fulton and Alan Fox in Ithaca, NY, May 23ʳᵈ, 2009

FOX: You said something that caught my attention: "Writing saves us from time."

FULTON: Oh, I don't know where I said that, but I think about time a lot, as a writer. It's that old thing about being in the moment and that through writing we can retrieve some of what we've lived and either relive it or allow other people to understand it. Also we can time travel in a way, through the imagination. And that's one of the powers of writing, I think, for me—more in fiction, I have to say, than in poetry. In poetry it's much more about ideas and language and feeling—and sometimes you get a little bit of narrative, of course you can, in poetry, because poetry can be anything. But when I think about time, I'm thinking more about narrative, I guess. In a way, though, poetry does the same thing.

FOX: It can.

FULTON: Because when we write it, it's there, and you've saved that moment, that feeling.

FOX: You've been published in *Best American Poetry* and also *Best American Short Stories*, which is rare. How do you compare the two in terms of your own writing?

FULTON: Well, it's very different, I think, although all writing comes from the same place. Writing poetry is, in a way, much more open, more free. You don't have to plan it as much as I've planned my short fiction—I've only written short fiction; I haven't written a novel. And because it's such a short form, the short story—I actually think it's the hardest form I've ever tried—I had to have some idea of where I was going, and I don't have that with poetry. Poetry to me is much more open and available to language and to the moment. Anything can be in a poem: you can have narrative, you can have ideas—it can be about ecology, botany, just anything and still be a good poem. With short fiction, really it's more about character and tension, something has to happen. Nothing has to happen in a poem. I love that about it—it can be interesting because of the language, the surface. And it's surprising, because you never know what it's going to do. Poetry—you just can't predict it. I think that's why people get hooked on poetry, because you realize suddenly you can put everything in it. Nothing is ruled out.

FOX: How do you go about writing? Do you have to be inspired, do you write at a certain time every day, when something strikes you...

FULTON: I find that if I sit down and think, "This is the time when I'm going to meditate or be contemplative," then something tends to come to me, while if I just waited for it to come without that process, nothing would come. Things are impinging all the time, driving away whatever one would write about. So I like to clear a space and say, "This is the time when I'm not going to deal with the world." Then things come to me. Things that have been smoldering begin to surface. So that's the approach. I don't think we can wait to be inspired. It's a luxury to think that's going to happen. [laughs] It's like waiting to be struck by lightning, as other poets have said, you know, you could go into that field a million times and not be struck by lightning [Fox laughs], but if you do certain things to yourself to make it more likely, stand under that big tree, then it could happen. You have to prepare the ground, let yourself be ready to write.

FOX: You say poetry is the most open form—do you censor yourself, either when you write or in showing your work to someone other than yourself?

FULTON: I don't, no. You know, there's a self-censor that you're not aware of— I mean, there's a part of me that's—yeah, I shouldn't be too quick about that, because there's a part of me that would reject certain phrases or lines. I might think, "Well, that's trite." Part of me might say, "That's boring, I'm not going to write that." But that's almost preconscious or subconscious; it's the part of me that's read a lot of poetry, the critic. But mostly it's a process of trying not to censor in that I want to get to things that are unbidden, things I haven't dared to say, things I've repressed, things I haven't acknowledged. The areas of my life or areas of human experience that make me uncomfortable are just the ones I would hope to go toward. And if I self-censor too much, I'd only write maybe the easier things.

FOX: Yes.

FULTON: So the censoring is more aesthetic, it's more "don't rhyme moon with June"—that's a crude example, but you know what I mean. It's an aesthetic censorship that develops over a lifetime of reading poetry. But in terms of the subject, the content, more and more I'm trying not to censor and to write what I think is real or what I'm really engaged with.

FOX: Are you ever concerned about offending someone?

FULTON: Not so much in poetry. It's a curious thing. Poets sometimes are. I've talked to other poets who've lost friends and whose relatives have gotten angry. But I guess I don't write poems right now that are about particular individuals. And usually what offends people is writing about them so they can identify themselves.

FOX: Yes.

FULTON: So I don't do that in poetry. In fiction, I think it's more of an issue because you're drawing on people you've known and there's always a chance that somebody would be offended or hurt by something, even if you change it as best you can. I've worried about that a lot more in fiction than I have in poetry.

FOX: In terms of the whole process, what part or parts of it do you enjoy the most—the actual writing, or talking with people about it, or teaching...

FULTON: I like all aspects of writing. It's a very good thing for me to do because it fits my temperament well. I like that it's quiet. I like that you're alone in a room. I like that it's contemplative. I like reading—all writers have to read a lot and I love to read. I like talking about it with other people. And I became a teacher, I think, originally because I was working in New York as a copywriter, writing advertising copy, my first job after college, and I had to use language in a way that felt very manipulative. My notion of becoming a teacher was that I could have my own salon; I could have my own gang. That was the dream, you've got this group, and you've all read the same book, and you're able to talk about it. It sounds like such a great thing to do. People have book groups now, of course, where they do this. Someone said when I was talking about this, "Well, why didn't you just start a book group?" And I said, "Well, I wouldn't have gotten paid for it." [Fox laughs] Because this is the fantasy, you can have your salon, your enthusiastic readers, all talking about the books, and you get paid for it. I thought it sounded like a really good gig. And it is.

I also like the sketchy part of writing where you feel everything is possible still, it still could be the greatest poem in the world. Of course by the time you finish it you realize what it is, and it's never quite what you wanted it to be, so that's why you write the next one. At its best, every aspect of being a writer is terrific. I never regretted being a writer, at all. I have many other regrets, but not that one. [laughs]

FOX: Ah. You reminded me, a friend of mine said years ago that "dreams are extremely fragile outside the womb of the mind."

FULTON: Yes. The possible.

FOX: What parts of writing can be taught and what, if any, can't be taught?

FULTON: I think writing comes from character, the writer's character. As a writer you bring everything you've lived to the page, so when I teach writing—mostly I teach poetry, I've only taught fiction once—it's coming from whatever the person has lived. You can teach a lot about aesthetics or technique and teach students how to become better readers, but in terms of what they actually write, it comes from the life they've lived, from what they've experienced, what they know. Flannery O'Connor said something like, "Anyone who doesn't have enough experience by the time they're eighteen will never be a writer."

FOX: Hm.

FULTON: As I've said to students, you could spend a lifetime trying to rewrite Yeats's poems and you never would, if only because you're in your generation, you're American. Students bring what they've lived, and it's very deep within them, although I can teach them other things, such as how to make the most of what they bring. That's why every student is different, and it's exciting to see what they can do.

FOX: Do you find that your students are open about themselves, or become more open as they write more?

FULTON: The older students are more open. The MFA students. They've made a commitment to being a writer and when you make that commitment you are naked in a way; you realize there's going to be a degree of exposure. What they don't realize yet is how criticism is going to feel with that exposure. It's as if someone comes along and tells you you're ugly. They don't have that part yet, but they do understand the commitment to honesty and to revelation. The younger students, the ones who are just beginning, are very concerned about the opinions of their peers in that little room around the table. They're embarrassed sometimes to say what they're feeling or write what's happened to them. So they can write something else now and come to that when they're ready to write it, later.

FOX: When I talked with Phil Levine, who teaches at Fresno State, which is kind of a working-person's college, he said he had taught for one semester a year at Princeton and I remember he was talking about the "What I did on my Spring Vacation" question, and he said the Princeton folks were just very superficial— "I went skiing, I did that"—and the students at Fresno State tended to be much more real, at least that was his experience. What is your experience along those lines with your students?

FULTON: Well, it's an interesting question, because I went to a place myself that was like Fresno, in a way. I went to Empire State College as an undergraduate. Speaking as a teacher I can only compare Cornell to other places I've taught, like University of Michigan, UCLA, and Berkeley. The Berkeley students often commuted from some distance, by bus. I'd give them an assignment from a book and they'd tear the pages out and bring them to class. I said, "What are you doing, tearing your books apart?" I love books so much, to me it's a sacrilege. [Fox laughs] I said, "Please don't tear the pages out of your books." But then one of the professors at Berkeley explained to me that the students have to carry a lot because they commute and they don't have any place to put the stuff. If they get there at seven in the morning, they're carrying books for their classes all day, and the books are just too heavy. So I thought, Okay. I never ran into that at Cornell, but alright, this is different. To get back to your question, I don't think that deep experiences, tragedy, things that are hard to write about or that need to be written about are the property of any one economic class. Cornell students are as thoughtful as any group I've taught, and so are Berkeley, UCLA, and Michigan students. They differ in more superficial ways. UCLA students would come to class barefoot sometimes, and of course there were film and theater majors, which was fun.

FOX: Well, Southern California tends to be much more informal than most places. I stopped wearing a tie years ago, except when I have to go to court occasionally. I just don't like ties. I'm often the only one without it. I had lunch with the CEO of my bank and there were fourteen people in the room, thirteen with suits and ties, and me with no suit and tie.

FULTON: Well, that's good.

FOX: I think so.

FULTON: Maybe everybody could loosen up a little. It might be catching, might be infectious. Show them the way! [laughs]

FOX: Absolutely. You've won many, many, many awards. How has that affected you as a person or a writer?

FULTON: That's very kind of you, but in truth, it doesn't seem like many to me! I wish there were more awards, for everybody, because I think it's great to win them. It gives you that little boost of confidence. You feel there's somebody out there who notices, there's someone listening, and it's certainly a good feeling. All writers who devote their life to literature and write good books should have awards. The biggest one I've had was the MacArthur fellowship. I had a wonderful experience learning about it. My husband and I were driving to Michigan from UCLA at the time. We were in Montana, and I called home—I hadn't spoken to my mother in weeks, so I called her and she said, "Did you hear the great news?" I said, "What do you mean? No." And she said, "You won a lot of money, you won an award!" and I said, "Well, what?" and she said, "Wait, I'll get the newspaper!" [Fox laughs] So my mother told me. She said, "You got this MacArthur thing," and I said, "Ah! No, it's not me, there's another Alice Fulton." I started screaming when she told me, but I couldn't believe it. I called the MacArthur Foundation, and the first thing they said was "Congratulations," so it was real. But it was wonderful that my mother was the one to tell me. Once I understood it was real, the shock and "what do you do next?" set in. How do you live up to it, how do you make the most of it, how do you not let this gift of time slip through your hands? You don't quite know how to feel, it's such a surprise. But of course it's very affirming. And I wish, I so wish, I fantasize, that there could be more things like that for writers. The MacArthur Foundation likes to support people somewhat earlier in their careers. I wish there was more support for people who have been writers all their lives. I think awards are terrific, and there should be more. There's no downside, as far as I can see.

FOX: Well, I suppose one downside, which is something you've talked about— you said, "I don't want to be smug." When did you figure that one out?

FULTON: This is going to sound smug, probably, but I don't think I've ever, as far as I know, had that tendency, because I'm somewhat insecure and self-critical. Also, you get the smugness knocked out of you by others. I guess that's the downside, actually, of something like the MacArthur—looking back you can say, "I should've done so much more, I could've done more"—there's always a comparison that can be made to someone who's more accomplished or prolific. The expectations are raised, and you can fail your own expectations. But as far as smugness goes, I don't know—I've probably had those moments, but I look back on them wishing I could have them again, because it must have been comfortable. To be complacent for a while would feel good.

FOX: Yes.

FULTON: It would feel nice to be able to say, "That went well didn't it?" To be able to relax and say, "I liked that, that worked." I haven't felt that way in a long time and I guess when I felt it I didn't know I was feeling it. Maybe people watching me were saying, "She seems too confidant, she seems too assured." But to me it just felt normal.

FOX: It seems to me that there's room for both. I mean, it's nice to feel good about yourself and your work, and I think it's also important if you want to do more work to be not smug and not satisfied.

FULTON: I think most writers probably aren't satisfied, because we're always thinking there's a greater work out there. And if you read a lot you can see so many great books, classics and contemporary books, have been written. I think as a writer you're always saying, "Well, I could've written something like that," or, "I want to write a book like that."

FOX: Yes. What do you see in your future in terms of writing? More of the same, or anything different?

FULTON: Oh, it's always different. I think each of my poetry books has been different from the previous one. Maybe there are poets who find a groove early on and stick with it. But I wasn't like that. I seem to be the other model: every book is trying to change or move forward, you could say, to do something different. What I'm interested in at the moment is invented languages. All poetry is an invented language anyway. You can see it in a poet like Emily Dickinson; she's a good example. You read Dickinson and it's English as a foreign language. Her work sounds like no English ever spoken anywhere, English from another planet. She took the language and made it deeply foreign, what she alone could do. The foreignness of poetry is interesting to me.

FOX: It seems to me that communication with language is uncertain, limited at best, full of noise, so maybe what you're talking about is trying to improve the communication by expanding or by different use of the language.

FULTON: Well, it's a strange thing because poetry doesn't exactly improve communication. It's full of noise, but the noise in poetry is beautiful noise. All of the disjunction, the slippage, the noise that's in poetry, becomes music. It's productive noise, something that we want to stay with and listen to. You may never understand it, but you want to listen to it. It's like music. You never can get to the bottom of it, and that's why you want to hear it again. With poetry you never can completely understand it, so it's an inherently imperfect communication. You don't have a relationship of perfect understanding, but the imperfection is part of the fascination. The ways that—oh, subtlety, and—ambiguity and mystery enter into poetry are probably its most important facets, the ways in which it isn't completely understood. A poet wants to hold on to the mystery, recognize when it's interesting and when it's not. It's a fine line between the boring, "yawn" stuff and the kind of poetry that draws you back because it's got something you want to reread even though you know you're never going to understand it completely.

FOX: Do you ever, when you've written a poem, look at it with a sense of surprise? "Did I know that?"

FULTON: I can remember that happening occasionally. Revisions—I'd look back and think, "Well, I don't know how that happened or where it came from, but it does seem to be what I want to write now that I see it, and it seems to be something I want to read." I'm always writing as a reader. I'm the reader *and* the writer.

FOX: Yes.

FULTON: I don't show my work to anybody, except my husband, before I send it out to an editor. After I write it, I become the reader. Then I can sometimes look at it and think, Yes, that's something I like to read. But sometimes I look back and I think, That wasn't my best moment. [Fox laughs] And even after it's published I'll sometimes look back and think, I don't know, that's not one of my favorites.

FOX: You've said that "one reader is an intimacy." Would you elaborate on that?

FULTON: There's something intimate about reading because it's done in a usually quiet room where the reader has time to think and pause and stop and imagine. It's unlike film, for example, movies, where people are often in a group and affected by the audience. Poetry readings are like that too. They're a performance, and as a listener at a poetry reading you're certainly affected by what other people are doing, just as at the movies you're affected by the audience—whether they laugh and clap.

FOX: Absolutely.

FULTON: But reading a book, it's really just a judge and jury of one. What will that one reader give you, how much slack will they cut for you, how much will they allow you of their time, their life, their mind? It's an honor when someone gives a book 10 hours, 60 hours, whatever it takes. And for me reading is such a deep pleasure. I do love watching film, but it's not the same as reading a book. Somehow when I'm reading the book I'm recreating it and it's more interactive. I have to engage with the book more, and I love that I can be quiet and close it and think and then open it again. And even the language I'm using is telling, the language of opening and closing and luxury and slowness. It's lascivious, it's erotic; reading is erotic because of the ways we can stop and start and go at our own pace. It's one of the deepest pleasures in the world, and I don't get enough of it anymore. This morning I was reading a book—actually it was Martin Amis, *House of Meetings*—I was just starting it and thinking, "Oh, it's wonderful to start this and close it and then come back to it." That is tantalizing.

FOX: Who are some of your favorite authors to read?

FULTON: Well, when I was writing short fiction, I didn't allow myself to read any prose except short fiction for a very long time, years. Now I'm starting to read novels again, which is wonderful—but in short fiction...gosh...Melanie Rae Thon, I like her work very much, and Edna O'Brian...I'm trying to think back...Annie Proulx...there are so many terrific fiction writers. Louise Erdrich, Carol Bly, Truman Capote, Doris Betts, Anthony Doerr, George Saunders, Joy Williams, Ha Jin, ZZ Packer... And with poetry, I'm just discovering lots of new poets who've only published one book: I'm always recommending them because students want to know who's just beginning. I think I'm seeing more good first books now than I've seen in twenty years.

FOX: Hm!

FULTON: There's so much more being published. There are so many presses now publishing work that tries to push the boundaries or take a risk. So I'm seeing a lot more that I find exciting in poetry. Kathleen Halme, Brian Henry, Emily Rosko, Theodore Worozbyt, Lara Glenum, Srikanth Reddy, Karen Leona Anderson, Charity Ketz, Dawn Lonsinger, to name just a few. And I also love a lot of poets I've been reading for ages—A.R. Ammons, of course, my teacher at Cornell. I'm afraid if I name others I'll leave people out! [Fox laughs]

FOX: You've also said that "embarrassment is intimacy for beginners." Say more about that.

FULTON: It seems that it's so hard to have intimacy these days because we're so much about self-presentation and façade. People learn the moves pretty quickly—I guess because as a culture we watch so much TV or movies. People learn to present themselves in ways that are polished. You used to see people doing commercials, for example, on TV, that were homemade—I remember this when I was an adolescent, a kid. You'd see them and they'd be absolutely wooden: "This is Eastman's Cheese House. We have the best cheese in upstate

New York." [Fox laughs] It would be absolutely wooden, they'd say "thee" for "the," "A—long A—A good place to get *thee* best cheese..." People were frozen in front of the camera. But now everybody's at ease, with technology, with the camera, the eye. There are cameras everywhere. So human reactions that are unscripted are becoming rare, and embarrassment can strip the façade away for a minute.

FOX: Yes.

FULTON: Very often, something embarrassing is an accident, something off-script. The unantipicated has happened, and all of a sudden you don't have the words, you don't have the moves, and the body begins to take over. You blush, you cry. And when you see someone embarrassed, you usually feel sorry for them, you want to say, "Oh, it's no big deal, it's really okay." There's compassion and a kind of intimacy because you're suddenly thinking, "Oh, you're human!" And the one it's happening to is feeling very human. So there's an acknowledgment of the human, I think, that we miss sometimes because we're trying to be perfect.

FOX: It seems that there's a deep human need for intimacy in the sense of being real with another person who's also being real, whether that's in person, which is probably the best, or in reading.

FULTON: You are so right. And I think that's very hard to find. It's hard to find people who are willing to talk about the things that are deep. I mean, that's what a friend is, really. With a friend you don't have to hide what you're really feeling, you can just say it. But it's rare. Very often people, I think, are afraid of what might happen, afraid of being drawn into some scenario that they don't want to get into. It's rare to find conversations where you can say what you're feeling and not feel judged or rebuffed, not feel that the other person is just bored—

FOX: Yes.

FULTON: —just, "I don't want to hear this, I don't want to listen to this." So when you find a friend, it's such a treasure.

FOX: Why do you think it's so rare?

FULTON: I think young people are better at friendship. I have friends from grade school and high school when we must have had less at stake. As adults, we often spend the most time with people who are working at the same job. When you're eighteen, you have a lot of energy and a lot of time, you can stay up all night and talk to each other until four in the morning about the deepest things. Once you have a family, responsibilities, a job, you're thinking, "I have to get up at seven to be at that meeting, I have to do this, I have to do that." You don't stay up until four o'clock in the morning talking to your friend the way young people do. So friendships just don't form in the way that they do when you're young. I wish it were different, because adults have so much to give, so much life experience.

FOX: Absolutely.

FULTON: They have more stories to tell and wisdom they could offer.

FOX: I think as you get older, we have a greater and greater investment in the status quo and maintaining that and not losing. So we see ourselves as having more to lose.

FULTON: Yes, yes.

FOX: And there's some truth to that, but then you lose a large part of the deepest pleasures of life.

FULTON: I guess that's what I was getting at with work friendships. They're hard because you're always worried that something is going to go wrong at the workplace, that what you say might get back to the wrong person, or if you confide, your colleague won't like you, and you have to go on seeing them for years. You're being more self-protective, while younger people maybe don't think so much that way.

FOX: Yeah.

FULTON: It's harder to make close friends I think as you go on in life. Have you made a lot of friends in the last, say, ten years that you think are very close?

FOX: Some, not—yeah, I would say so, two or three, which I regard as very good.

FULTON: That's *very* good, yeah.

FOX: I kind of think of my life as 80 percent "I want the status quo and the familiar and the comfortable" and then 20 percent "I want new and exciting and adventure and vibrant."

FULTON: That's probably a very healthy balance, actually.

FOX: I do it that way; I'm not saying it's right or wrong, but that's what tends to work for me. Do you think a writer has to be contemplative in terms of their own process, for a poet?

FULTON: I think so. Now, some poets are more sociable than others. Some poets are party animals. And some are poeticians: they work the room. But I think even people who are very adept at the social aspects have to be somewhat contemplative or they couldn't write the poems. You've got to be able to go inward. There are people I've found, and it's surprised me, who can't do that at all. I guess they'd never be writers. There are people who need distractions. They can't be alone because too much would come out that they don't want to think about. They can't do what writers do, which is to be alone and confront whatever it is. You've got to like that process. It can't be something you're afraid of or something you don't want to do.

FOX: Absolutely. Three themes that you've talked about are altruism, love and loneliness. I'd like you to say more about each of those.

FULTON: Oh, you've been reading my interviews, that's really nice of you. I think I talked about those things when I was describing my fiction collection [*The Nightingales of Troy*]. That book is in part about the limits of altruism in the characters' lives—how much can each of them give? Some give too much and some thrive on caring for others—a nurse character, for instance. It's a fine line—how much can you give before you've become a masochist? What's the line between masochism and altruism? I believe in altruism, but how much can you give before you starve? How much nourishment can you give away before there isn't enough to nourish yourself? It's a big question, especially for teachers, because you're giving others the same stuff that you need for yourself, in a way—the same time, the same energy. How to negotiate that? How to understand it?

Loneliness is—oh, gosh, I always find it moving when I hear the pop songs about loneliness. Only pop songs seem to be able to talk about it. For instance, a great song, Billie Holiday's "Solitude": "In my solitude, you haunt me." Loneliness is feeling that your experiences are inexpressible or unshared by anyone, that you'll never be able to make anyone understand what you've been through. I think that's partly why people become writers, out of a need to explain experiences so well that someone else can nod their head and say, "I know what you mean, I understand it." And then the writer feels less lonely. You feel, well, it was awful, but somebody out there will understand what I went through. I think it's a profound reason to write, that loneliness. When you write it, other people say, "I've felt that too, and you've articulated it for me," the way that Billie Holiday, when she sings that song, says it for me, or sings it for me. She sings with such yearning. The other abstraction—let's see, it was altruism, loneliness and you had a third—

FOX: Love.

FULTON: Oh, love. God—love is—love is so painful and it's a compound of many other emotions, it's not simple—it is partly loneliness because if you love someone you're always separate. Even though you love them there's always the air between you that leaves you alone. And love is the most difficult thing to attain, I think. When you love someone you want to spare them suffering, you want to protect them, and you want to be with them. But in the end, sometimes you can't protect them, you can't spare them, and you can't be for them what you wanted to be. I think with kids you would know what I mean. I'm thinking about this in relation to my mother, too. I was her caregiver when she was quite old. I wanted to protect her because I loved her. I wanted to save her, and in the end I was just helpless. Love makes you helpless. You try and try but because of human limitations, we can never be perfect. I guess that's why everyone says it's the deepest emotion—it's the one we're least equal to, I think.

Fox: I remember a movie I saw many, many years ago, *Carnal Knowledge*, where it started out with a black screen and two characters talking and one of them asked a question which has stayed with me ever since, which was, "Is it better to love or to be loved?" How would you...

Fulton: I think we need both desperately. It's probably 50/50. We need to be able to love because it makes everything deeper, more beautiful and profound. It makes life meaningful. But also you have to be loved. Maybe not by the person you're loving; it doesn't have to be reciprocal—I think you can give love to one person and get it from another and maybe that works out okay as long as you're getting love from somewhere. But you need to feel that someone values you. Maybe the rarer thing is to be loved. It's hard to feel loved, and people often don't feel it. They don't feel that they're loved.

Fox: Mm, perhaps feel unworthy, or there's an obligation there...

Fulton: Unappreciated...

Fox: Sure. Do you think age is a part of this? In terms of altruism, for example—and I know we all have to preserve ourselves; if you don't preserve yourself, as you say, if you give away all your food and starve, that's not what many people would do. But on the other hand, as I get older, it's very clear to me, just on a feeling basis, that we are here to help each other. I think that's very, very important. And so my own view has changed a lot since I was eighteen and probably more selfish than most, extremely selfish—I probably still am on some levels. But do you think age affects that?

Fulton: Altruism...I think I always believed in it, but the clichés are true, experience makes you wiser, it makes you calmer, you are able to advise people better, you're less emotional; you have more equipoise, equilibrium. You're able to give more to others if you're more balanced yourself. And maybe when you're young you're so torn by love, finding a life partner, getting through it, that you don't have much left to give. Later, you can look at younger people and say, "I know what that's like and maybe I can even do something to help you."

Fox: I would agree with that. Daveen, do you have anything?

Daveen: It seems to me that much of what you've been talking about is being filled up yourself in order to be able to give; if you're empty, you don't have the food, the energy, the ideas. So how do you get filled up, personally?

FULTON: It just takes time. Instead of filling, it's as if I have to empty out. It takes time with nothing in it for me to be empty enough, peaceful enough. The world is always impinging, filling us in a way, but what I need is to clear it out and not think about it, to have a sense of space, a sense of the blank slate, the blank piece of paper. Then there's a feeling of possibility, no lid—nothing pressing down, open space. There's an openness I can *be* in, luxuriate in. There's no pressure. For me, that's it. What it takes is getting rid of obligations, the letters of recommendation, the meetings. I don't mean this meeting, I mean tedious, obligatory meetings. All of that obligation stuff has to be out of the way for me. It's a terrible way to be. Writers are lucky if they can compartmentalize. I'm not like that. I'm not at all like that. I can't do it. The writers who get up at five or six and then write until eight and then go teach? I envy them. I've tried to do it; I keep trying again and again. But I'm not like that, I'm permeable. If I've got something later in the day, it's already with me at five in the morning. I wake up with it in my head, it's there, and I'm not going to be able to get rid of it. So I need space, whether it's—a day would be the minimum; it's better to have months, and then I can go more deeply into that space. Afterwards it's like coming up from the subterranean. You think, Where am I? You've been into the imagined world so deeply. I think the way I do it isn't good. It's just my temperament. Again, writing comes from temperament, from character, and people don't get to choose. Maybe there's a good side to it, but it certainly slows me down, because I can't just push everything away. That's why artist colonies exist. They're trying to give you a sanctuary—but if you've ever been to them, there you are at dinner with all these people you've never met, making conversation, which can be very disruptive. To find the perfect space with nothing in it except thinking and words and books is very, very hard.

DAVEEN: You often mention meditation—you do that as a preamble, or...

FULTON: I used to. I've never done it regularly. This pillow you asked me about is from the Zen Temple in Ann Arbor. I took a course there for six weeks. I did learn about meditation. But I think writing is meditation for me. It is contemplative. And what we learned at the Zen Temple was breathing; it was "concentrate on the breath, just breathe, and don't think at all, just breathe." That's helpful to me when I'm in various situations that are difficult. But as a poet, I go inwards and try to reach the deepest thing I can encounter through language. I don't have to think about people. With fiction you really do, but with poetry, there are no people, there's just you and language. I read a quote from Sonia Sanchez the other day. She said, "The language loved me and I loved it back." I thought, What a beautiful line. But I don't think it's true for me; I never felt language loved me, but I did love it. And that gets back to your question about love—I do love language deeply, but I can't feel that sense of reciprocity. Language is too wily. Language, as we all know, can be used in vile, mean, terrible, nasty ways. So language is not all nice, and when I'm writing I'm dealing with aspects of language that aren't good, too, parts that are corrupted and ugly, because I'm trying to encompass as much as I can, to let as much into the poetry as possible, and I think about language doing things that are unbeautiful as well as beautiful. Language is power. It's different from meditation because it's socially inflected. You find yourself thinking, "This is a word from the Gulag, this is from a very dark place, this particular word." Language is political as well as transcendent.

FOX: Well I think one good thing about your not being compartmentalized is your self-awareness. Maybe you want to be seven feet tall and you're not—okay, deal with it. We all have to deal with who we are, with our abilities and limitations, and that's what you have to work with.

FULTON: That's exactly right. There's a wonderful book by a Buddhist nun—Pema Chodron—called *Start Where You Are*. It's a fine directive. You've got to forget that you did it wrong yesterday. You have to play the hand you're dealt, begin with what you're given and make the most of it.

FOX: Absolutely. Well, I think we're fine.

FULTON: I hope I gave you something.

FOX: What I was thinking toward the end is that you're the—I'd be extreme about this, I'd say you are the only *pure* poet that I've talked to.

FULTON: Oh my gosh, I don't even know what you mean by pure. [laughs]

FOX: I'm not sure either. You are all this, the language and the love and the altruism—

FULTON: Well, thank you, that's a very sweet compliment. One of my favorite sayings from Emily Dickinson is, "I find I need more veil." Of course, literally in the nineteenth century, they did veil—but she meant it metaphorically, that she needed more cushion, boundary, she needed some screen. And all my life I've felt that I needed more veil. Everything gets in and I have no way to keep it out. In a way that's helpful, but in another way it's dangerous. I'm also too honest. Pathologically honest.

FOX: Yes, but you almost certainly don't have a choice.

FULTON: Right. You can try to have more facade—which is another of my obsessions, facade and covering—you can try to build it up, but in the end it's pretty impossible. There's always a way to get through the chinks.

FOX: Yes. I've always had that problem, and one of the things is superficiality—I mean, I see people at parties and they enjoy themselves and are having a great time, it's totally superficial, and part of me says, Gosh, I wish I could do that.

FULTON: Yes.

FOX: And I can't. I just can't.

FULTON: I can't either. I'm not a party person at all. I'm awful at large gatherings, they scare me. I have to steel myself to go into a party and then I'm the one who gloms onto one person [laughs] because I'm afraid to go around and talk to the others. I'm very bad at that kind of social thing and I've never become much better.

FOX: I did it once. Once when I was single, the woman I was dating invited me to a wine-tasting party and I decided I would talk to the people at the party superficially for ten minutes and then I would excuse myself and go on to somebody else. And I talked to nineteen people, I had nineteen very successful superficial conversations and I proved to myself that I *can* do it. Didn't like it, never done it since, but...

FULTON: [laughing] Well, that makes me feel better. Maybe if you find someone who's interesting, you should let it play out and see how it goes.

FOX: That's what I tend to do, absolutely.

FULTON: I'm the same way. I have found—and this is maybe not for the interview—but just lately I've been noticing that I don't cry anymore. I'm feeling that tears are on the surface and there's something deeper that can't be accessed. The one thing that gets to me is music. It's as if it infiltrates my nerves. It goes between the synapses and into the nervous system where nothing else can reach. It gets at whatever's so down deep, and then I begin to feel. Lyric poetry can have that power, too, a sublime power that—almost inexplicably—reaches within and moves us.

A CONVERSATION WITH MOLLY PEACOCK

portrait by Lara Tomlin

MOLLY PEACOCK is the author of six volumes of poetry, including *The Second Blush* and *Cornucopia: New & Selected Poems*, both published by W.W. Norton and Company (US and UK) and McClelland and Stewart (Canada). Her poems have appeared in leading literary journals such as *The TLS*, *New Yorker*, *Nation*, *New Republic*, and *Paris Review*, as well as in numerous anthologies, including *The Best of the Best American Poetry* and *The Oxford Book of American Poetry*. She is the Series Editor for *The Best Canadian Poetry* in English and serves on the Graduate Faculty of the Spalding University Brief Residency MFA Program in Creative Writing.

Conversation Between Molly Peacock and Alan Fox in Brentwood, CA, October 27th, 2008

FOX: Molly, you've used the phrase, "the shimmering verge," a lot. What's the essence of that?

PEACOCK: The phrase pops up in the last chapter of my book, *How to Read a Poem and Start a Poetry Circle* and "The Shimmering Verge" became the title of my one-woman stage show. The shimmering verge, for me, is the place between two states of being or two emotions. I opened my show by asking people to imagine a green paint chip. Then I asked them to imagine a blue paint chip, then to imagine one greenish-blue and one blueish-green and greenish-greenish-blue and blueish-blueish-green until they couldn't tell the difference. That is the shimmering verge, the place where one color shifts into the other and you can't figure out exactly where. That's analogous to where one emotional state shifts into the other, but you can't figure out exactly where. For me, this in-between place is where the poem occurs.

The poem is always about the thing we initially don't have words for: that's why the poem exists. There are ordinary states like that shimmer, for instance, the state when you don't know whether to leave or stay, when you don't know whether you love the person or hate the person, or when you don't know whether to be thrilled or afraid or whether to laugh or cry. That's a kind of shock state, and there's an element of a shock in the shimmering verge as well—it's quieter than all-out shock, but that's what I'm talking about. It's not that there isn't a border, it's that you can't quite tell where it is, like where the side of a road exactly ends and the land begins. It's that kind of thing—where the lake ends and the shore begins. It's those kinds of external and internal verges that I'm talking about.

FOX: And you said that a poem is from a state that you can't put into words.

PEACOCK: Mmhmm—

FOX: And yet you do put it into words—

PEACOCK: That's the poet's job: to take the wordless state and articulate it. I feel like it's my job, at any rate. And when I consider something as a subject for a poem, that's kind of the position that I'm in. "What is it, what is it? It's eluding me; I can't quite grasp it." There's something ineffable about the subject for the poem, even if it's a pink paper clip. What is it about the pink paper clip that would draw me so that I feel the need to write about it?

FOX: Many poets have talked about music or jazz as being akin to poetry. It seems to me in terms of expressing emotion, maybe it's easier in music, or painting, than it is in words.

PEACOCK: Well, music is perhaps the most purely emotional art in that it doesn't have to "articulate" anything. And painting creates the image. And those are two arts that I feel are tucked inside poetry. When we talk about the vision of the poet, we can liken that to painting, and that's where we get ideas of word-painting. The music of the poem is—well, there are two musics in the poem: there's the music of the line, which I think of as like a bassline, if we're still in the jazz mode—so there's that bassline going; and then there's the music of the sentence, quite separate, it's prose music. People who only pay attention to the music of the sentence get accused of writing chopped-up prose, but there is a distinct sentence music that unfolds over the lines. Those two rhythms—the bassline rhythm beneath each line as well as the rhythm of the sentence wrapping around the lines—combine to create deep emotional states. Because the music comes almost from a preverbal place, sometimes, as poets, we're not even consciously aware of what those emotions connote. But when we talk about the vision of a poet, I think actually we're talking about a poet's imagery—or what the poet paints. When we say, "Wallace Stevens' vision" or "William Carlos Williams' vision" or "Elizabeth Bishop's vision" or "Sonia Sanchez's vision," I think we're largely talking about what they *en*vision in their imagery.

FOX: You're known as a new formalist—

PEACOCK: Yeah...[laughs]

FOX: [laughing] Why do you laugh at that?

PEACOCK: [laughing] At this point I feel a little bit like an old formalist! But, yes.

FOX: Well, how does formalism enter into your writing for you, in terms of the vision, the imagery, all that?

PEACOCK: I'm a psychological formalist, how's that? My interest in formal poetry started because I began with too-hot-to-handle subject matter. I was in psychological states that were just flooding me with feeling and language, and I didn't know what to do with them. I didn't want just to vomit something out on a page, yet I wanted to write deeply personally. I wasn't interested in abstraction at all when I started off writing. I just was too consumed by feeling. Being overwhelmed was what drew me to formal boundaries. Most people think of form as being the outside of something. For instance your high school teacher might tell you that a sonnet is like an empty vase, a container you pour the poem into. My professor at Johns Hopkins, the eminent poet Richard Howard, kept telling me it was the inside of something, not the outside. From this idea I leapt to my own thought about poetic form as a skeleton, the bones inside the body of a poem, not external to the poem at all. If I knew how to use formal devices, I thought, then I could infuse them with what was overwhelming me, and I would be making art at the same time. I wanted to make art, and for me, a formal poem is an art object, made with precision. When I see a sculpture, say, a brass sculpture that is highly polished, or a wood sculpture that someone sanded again and again and again, hundreds of times returning to it to get the sheen of its surface—that's the kind of art object that I'm talking about.

And I probably don't have to tell you that my sensibility is extremely visual, as you've no doubt figured out by my analogies—I'm starting off with a paint chip, for crying out loud! As a child I drew and painted, but words, I suppose, the articulation of something, became more important to me. But I've always had a lust for the visual, and my thinking tends toward the image.

Another aspect of formal poetry that drew me to it is that it ensured a kind of musicality. And formal poetry also addressed the inadequacies I felt about class. I'm a working-class girl from Buffalo, New York. I'm the first person in my family to go to college. I wanted to write "real poetry" and someone from a more sophisticated background would've understood that they could've broken all kinds of boundaries in poetry, but I wanted to be certified as a real poet and to me that meant the poets that you read in school—where else did I read them? They certainly weren't at home; no one there was talking about them. So, that meant being able to do what John Keats and John Donne did. It meant—it's bizarre to call Keats a formalist; he did what he did as a poet, not a so-called formalist. But I thought I needed to be able to work in rhyme and meter in order to be the real thing. Then if I wanted to throw verse structures away, of course I could do it later, when I'd become grand and sophisticated and educated. But I had to learn it first.

FOX: Isn't that kind of like an artist learning the classical-style perspective, then they can go to abstract if they want to—

PEACOCK: Yes, absolutely, absolutely. I think it's just like studying figuration—all that Renaissance gray under-painting before they put the color on, stuff like that. We're always connecting with the past, and one of the ways we connect with the past is through technique. This is also psychological for me as well, a way of constructing an artistic family tree. You cannot choose your family. You're given your family. But as you become a poet, you begin to choose your poetic family. You get to discover your literary aunts and uncles and the writers you're related to. And it can be a very disparate family. The older you get, the larger the family becomes, and the more you read, the more poets you encounter from around the world, or poets you rediscover and discover that they were part of your family after all—the interconnectedness is part of what draws me to formal technique.

FOX: Wouldn't it be fair to say also that you find you can better communicate that flood of emotion through more formal imagery than another way?

PEACOCK: Well, it's not exactly that the imagery is formal. It's that the rhythms of the language and the sound system is formal. That's really what it is. And then the imagery can be bizarre. I have a poem called "Anger Sweetened" in which there's a strange image of a candied grasshopper (like chocolate ants only this is a grasshopper dripping with caramelized sugar). It's a terrifying image, and when it came into my head, I thought, Ugh, *this horrifies me*. But it horrified me so much that I had to seek it out. I realized that it was an image of holding back your anger and kind of candying your words, and I ended up writing a sonnet about that called "Anger Sweetened." That's an example of using a weird, dream-like image, not a "formal image" of something genteel, but more of a film image inside the formal poem.

FOX: Is what you're trying to get at a deeper communication than we normally would have in a social setting?

PEACOCK: I'm interested in the surfaces of things, but I'm not interested in the superficial. [laughs]

FOX: Ah, what's the distinction?

PEACOCK: By surfaces I might mean I'm interested in—how can I say—the textures of life. The glass texture, or the texture of fabric, and that's social fabric as well, but I'm not so interested in being— There's a wonderful kind of poetry that comes from making chattiness an art. This is a kind of so-called superficiality that I adore—but it's not me. Even though I'm a hearty laugher and my poems can be quite funny, at root they're about some bell that resounds deep inside me that's very serious.

FOX: What kind of reaction would you want from your readers?

PEACOCK: I want them to say, *Yes, I've felt that too. Yes, I knew that somewhere inside me but I never would've put it that way, and that's a revelation to me.* So I'm hoping for the response of my reader to be an affirmation and a revelation. And thank you for asking that question [laughs] and provoking my answer because I've never been asked that question before. I mean, that's very nice to discover.

FOX: You talk about ambiguity. Why don't you elaborate on that?

PEACOCK: Let's begin with the opposite of ambiguity—the transparent emotions of childhood. Childhood has—we might even define childhood through the purity of its emotional states. There's no fear purer than childhood fear, there's no thrill purer than childhood thrills, there's no discovery as palpably delicious as the discoveries we make in childhood, and part of that sense of purity is that the occurrences are unambiguous, that the pleasure's whole, that the horror's unmitigated. As we begin to grow up, experiences begin to repeat. With this comes the phenomenon of feeling two things at once, of having co-existing responses, even if it's only the past response recalled within the present one. This layering of experience makes life ambiguous. For me, art veers between these two ideas—at least my art veers between these two states of clarity and ambiguity. There's a part of me that just loves going after the limpid image.

When I first began writing, I had an image in my mind for how I wanted the poem to be: a lake that had no sediment in it, so that in reading the poem you would be looking straight down into the bottom, that it would have that kind of supreme clarity, and yet it was clarity that came as a surprise because it resulted from looking at something through water, though another medium. And I don't necessarily have that image now, but I kind of think that in the beginning my work as a poet meant going after those pure childhood states through another medium: words.

As I've matured I've gotten more interested in the ambiguous states. But I do feel that that tension exists in me as an artist; clarity is what I'm drawn to, but as I become more of a fossil [all laugh], I can't help but write out of the sort of astonishment at the multiple layers of experience that I have when I react to anything now. All those multiple layers are invoked, and I'm compelled to speak through all of them.

However, I look forward to the simplicity of my late period. I love artists' late periods, and this profound simplicity they seem to attain. I aspire to it. [laughs]

FOX: Isn't that sort of back to the purity of the poem...

PEACOCK: I think it is, I think it is.

FOX: Well, that's a good point. I understand that you work privately with poets. What do you generally work on with them?

PEACOCK: The history of my working one-to-one with emerging poets is also kind of...socially and economically and culturally interrelated. When I got my MA from The Johns Hopkins Writing Seminars in 1977, typically young poets would get one-year jobs in some place and then immediately they'd have to apply for their next one-year jobs. I had friends who'd go to Morningside, Iowa and then they'd be in Wichita, Kansas and then they'd be in...no offense to Morningside, or Wichita for that matter, but they were not necessarily places that drew me. [laughs] And I thought to myself, I can't live like that; how can I make art if I'm constantly on the move? I travel constantly now but I do have one home [laughs] when I get to it. So I decided to pick the place, not let the job determine the place. I picked New York where I could live a literary life outside of academe.

That's how I became involved in The Poetry Society of America and Poetry In Motion, and also how I ended up teaching 7th grade at a Quaker school, Friends Seminary, which also was very stable for me. I'm glad that I did it; I was there for eleven years. But I also knew I just couldn't teach 7th grade forever, and I studied to become a learning-disabilities specialist. I didn't finish that degree, and I didn't actually go into a career as a learning-disabilities specialist, but I did develop a small private practice with children. At the same time people started to bring me manuscripts—and this was New York, and New York is a place with a huge service culture. I mean, you go to people and pay them for consults for anything you could possibly imagine. When people with manuscripts approached me, I would explain that I wasn't a university professor holding open office hours, but that if I could fit the person into my practice, I would. I would say something like, "If you come at a certain time, I'll talk to you about your poems for that hour, but I would have to charge you what I would charge a child's family for that hour." And the writers said, "Fine." It's the kind of thing where, in another part of the country, people might be horrified, but in New York it was just part of the commerce of everyday life. And so, that's how I started working with poets one-to-one. Usually, my students would bring me poems, and we would talk about them, and these lessons developed into manuscript consults for whole books. I've done that for…oh my gosh, maybe 25 years. This has meant long, long-lasting relationships, sometimes through two or three books. These have been deep, sometimes profound, relationships that have gone on over time.

This is how I became interested in brief residency MFA programs. I've used similar techniques where I now teach at the Spalding University Brief Residency MFA Program.

FOX: Do you ever consult with anybody about your own work?

PEACOCK: I do. I have a friend, Phillis Levin, the poet, author of *Mercury* and *Mayday,* published by Penguin and editor of *The Penguin Book of the Sonnet.* Phillis and I went to Johns Hopkins together. Since the fall of, I think, 1976, we have seen every poem the other has written. It's really a long time. And we have talked about one another's work, and each of us has been the lens through which the other person has seen for all these years. I can't imagine what my poems would look like without her in many ways, even though our sensibilities are completely different. We don't make a demand on one another in terms of sensibility; that's really not what we do. Every writer needs another eye. But I've been lucky enough to have an intense, reflective relationship with someone, a friendship, that's really based on poetry. We're friends in all other aspects of our lives, of course, but this is the core of our friendship.

FOX: Do you ever find either of you being defensive about the poems?

PEACOCK: Nope. It's a miracle, and I don't know how it works. No. There are things, predilections that we have, and predispositions that we have, and I know that Phillis will land on certain ideas in a poem. But we give each other a wide berth about that sort of thing. And I don't think we're really holding back, it's just that we know certain things about one another, so we wouldn't press on something—it's kind of like if you have a bunion, you don't buy a pair of shoes that exacerbates the pain from your bunion. [laughs] It's that kind of thing. And yet we still after all these years surprise each other with our insights.

FOX: You mentioned "Poetry In Motion." Tell me about that.

PEACOCK: Well, it's the most fun, most effective volunteer poetry project of my life. And I did it with Elise Paschen, who was the executive director of the Poetry Society of America and two lovely men at the New York Transit Authority, the now long-retired president of the subway system, Alan Kiepper, and a man who worked deep within the administrative bowels of the transit system, Neil Neches. Elise and I had wanted to put poetry on the New York City subways because Elise saw the poems on the London subways, and my old professor at Binghamton University, Milton Kessler, urged me to make a similar program. We kept trying to find a way through the mandarin hierarchy of the New York City transit system, and we weren't being very successful. Then we tried to find funding, and we weren't very successful. Through a friend, though, Elise heard that Alan Kiepper wanted to do this. Then we realized that there are just a handful of men—I don't know, nine men maybe in the world—who run major subway systems. Just think of it, there's the Tokyo guy, the London guy, the New York guy, and they get together—of course, why wouldn't they? What a very select group, I don't think there's a woman among them—and they're envious of one another. Each one wants for his subway what his rivals have. Kiepper, who loved Robert Frost's poetry, was jealous that London had a poetry program. So you might say that a combination of rivalry and Robert Frost got the New York program going. We were young and adorable when we met Kiepper, and we said, "You can't just have Ogden Nash on the subways, you know!" [all laugh] "We love Ogden, but we need more than that, we need Shakespeare, and we need Robert Frost." [laughs] And he said, Okay, girls, you go ahead and choose the poems, dears, and we'll put them up. So that's the anecdotal version of how it began.

FOX: When did that start?

PEACOCK: Seventeen years ago, in 1992.

FOX: Whoa. Is it still happening?

PEACOCK: Well, it's happening in cities around the country. It is not so much happening in New York, actually, because now other aspects of intellectual culture have realized the importance of putting words on the subway, so now we have words of wisdom from philosophers and all kinds of other people, along with the occasional poem.

FOX: You've encouraged poetry circles. Tell me about that.

PEACOCK: Poetry is a solitary art, and often it's read in solitude, but as we know through your investigations of slam poetry culture and poetry-reading culture, there's also a social aspect to it. I've been in a book group for many, many years. There are only four of us, and we live in different cities, and we get together occasionally; it's not one of those every-month book groups. This group inspired me, as well as the classes I teach at the 92nd Street Y in New York, where people just want to come and read poetry—but to read it with some guidance. So I realized I was engaged in forming poetry circles, in an organic way. Then I began thinking that, you know—that was happening at the same time as I was, I have to say, a bit disaffected with poetry workshops, that the dynamic in poetry workshops wasn't, from my point of view, the healthiest, nor did it lead to a deeper connection with the practitioners of the art. You'd meet with a poetry workshop, and no one would expect you to bring in a poem from a real poet, a great poet, another poet who wasn't in the workshop. In reaction I began bringing a lot of literature into my workshops, and that also laid the ground for the poetry circles. When the workshop participants all had something really fantastic to focus on, the level of the writing just elevated almost instantly.

All of those things came together, and I wrote a book called *How to Read A Poem and Start a Poetry Circle*, and it had a nice little life out there. It was published just after I published a memoir, and it was kind of a bit of a—it was another place for my mind to go after I exhausted myself on the memoir.

Fox: You've also, I think, written about not having children. Can you say something about that?

Peacock: Yes, I have, especially in my memoir, *Paradise, Piece By Piece*. I really made a choice not to have children, and I don't even know whether young women feel the need to make such a choice anymore. But where I was in life, back to that working-class house in Buffalo, and my dad, a kind of deteriorating alcoholic, and my mom—her way of coping was to flee, not formally abandon us, but more on a daily basis. She had a little grocery store, and she was in this store from ten in the morning to ten at night. At the age of twelve I became the mainstay of the household in terms of getting my sister to do her homework, ironing my father's shirts, cooking dinner, and doing all of that domestic stuff. I had the work of a mother without the pleasures of motherhood, and in some ways the work of a wife, but without any sort of boundary blurring in terms of sexuality, yet I performed housewife-y functions. Plus I went to school and tried to have a life of my own. There was a lot on my plate, and I hated it.

Really, I *hated* all of those responsibilities. Partly I hated them because I wasn't very good at them. I wasn't good at cooking dinner, I wasn't good at ironing shirts—which I still don't do, I won't do! [all laugh] I married a man who wouldn't dream of asking me!

And my sister was wild, much wilder than I was, and I was terrible at controlling her. So it was a disaster. What I wanted was: *out*. Many people in that situation want to recreate a family; they think, *When I have my family, it's not going to be like this.* My reaction was, I don't want to have anything to do with families. I want to be an artist and I want to make art. And I want out.

Most younger women in North America (just to broadly generalize!) feel that they can have both the journey *and* the nest—I wanted the journey. I knew this very young, but I could hardly say it. Frankly, it was easier to say in the sixties and early seventies than it is now. The Right has commandeered all of the language about choice and women's choices and about women's lives, and I fervently hope that in a couple weeks that's going to change. [Note: This interview took place just before the 2008 Presidential election.] My memoir was published in 1998, and I think if I were bringing that manuscript around now, ten years later, it would have a tougher time.

Your circumstances shape your life. We all feel—how can I say it?—if you're a North American, you just feel you can do anything, that your life is governed by free will. But if you look closely at your life, you find that it's governed by all kinds of limits. Part of those limits, for me, were emotional. I was a fully formed mini-adult at a very young age, so I looked and acted as though I were capable of handling all the responsibility that was thrust at me, but inside I was almost unformed. I just really didn't have a chance to grow up. That growing had to happen much later in my life. I have an extremely happy mid-life marriage, and I look at my husband now and think, *Oh, he would have made a marvelous father.* I still don't think I would have made such a marvelous mother! [laughs] It's the truth; I'm too erratic. But he has a fabulous steadiness about him, the kind of steadiness that you need in a household bringing up children. So, it's not that I don't have sadness about what I haven't done in my life, but I still can't say that I have profound regret. I've had a truly wonderful life, and I'm grateful for it. I'm deeply grateful for it.

FOX: It sounds to me like you found your niche and occupied it, which is something that certainly not everyone can say.

PEACOCK: That's for sure. I should say that there was the help of a good therapist in there, too. [laughs]

FOX: That can be helpful. Professionally, Molly, what gives you the most pleasure?

PEACOCK: Oh, writing. I do a bit of acting. I write prose. I write poetry. But I would say that my deepest pleasure comes from writing poetry. Even though I do write quite a bit of prose, and I like it, and I can't imagine life without prose, nor can I imagine my life without some aspects of performance, but really I'm happiest in my bathrobe writing a poem. [laughs]

FOX: Was there a moment in which you had a flash of inspiration that you're a poet, as opposed to a playwright, or another kind of writer?

PEACOCK: No. As a child, I wanted to be something special, but I didn't know what the special thing was.

FOX: You mentioned that you were disaffected with poetry workshops. Say more about that.

PEACOCK: It's not that I don't think that people can learn a lot in poetry workshops; I do think they can. But I also feel that there's a kind of unstable rhetoric in a poetry workshop. People say things to the poet under discussion like, *Oh, I would've liked it if you would've done blah blah.* And that's not the point! It's not about what another person happens to prefer! Or someone whines, *I wanted to hear more about such and such.* And then I think, Wait a minute, it's not about what you wanted to hear, it's about what this writer is trying to write. As a fellow participant in the workshop you have to climb out of yourself and climb behind the writer under discussion and look through that person's eyes and try to help them through their goals. This is an extremely difficult thing to do because workshops require the students to develop their skills as writers as well as to develop their critical skills. The problem is, they're honing their critical skills on other student work! That puts too big a burden both on the nascent critic and on the poor person who is the subject of those inchoate critical skills. It's a very tough situation; it requires a lot of teaching. A teacher really has to be very, very active to make it all work. I am an active workshop teacher, but it is a fraught situation.

I love my one-to-one teaching both at Spalding and on my own because I feel like I'm reaching into an endless bag of responses for each person: try this, try that, read this person, try this technique. I attempt to be full of responses to them, and it frees me from the psychosocial dynamic of the workshop, and it frees the student to feel a student's vulnerability. I do teach workshops, I'm not totally against them; I just feel that they're fraught with difficulties.

FOX: What advice would you give to a young, aspiring student?

PEACOCK: Oh, to keep doing it. To persist. To persist and to know that they don't have to develop a so-called thick skin. People have a mistaken idea about rejection—they advise younger writers, You have to develop a thick skin about your rejection. And I say the true poet never has a thick skin; the poet depends on having a thin skin, a very thin membrane between the poet and the world. And you are going to be hurt by rejection, and it doesn't get better, it gets different as you get older—largely because you usually know the person who's rejected you, you have a personal relationship with your rejector. [laughs]

You somehow have to accept about yourself the fact that there is only that kind of thin boundary between you and the world, and that you have to protect yourself. One of the ways you can best protect yourself is to write, and to write a lot. I'm not the kind of person who insists to young writers that they have to write at the same time every day. I don't myself; I could hardly advise people to do that. But it's good to write a lot, and then you're not obsessively revising one perfect thing all the time.

FOX: One final question, especially in lieu of our interruption earlier, how has becoming well-known and all that affected your life?

PEACOCK: It's lovely to walk into a room and have people know who you are. This is the wonderful state of being known but not famous—and that's where I am: I'm not a famous poet—I'm a known poet. But there's a lovely feeling about that recognition, about someone saying, *Oh I know your work*, or, *I've known your work for years*, or that sort of thing, and I'm very gratified by it. I don't really think there's a downside—I think there's a downside to being famous, but I don't think there's a very big downside to being known. It's an extremely pleasant state to be. But I have to say that it's put a lot more travel into my life and I'm busier than I would like to be, and I'm not very good at sorting it all out. I am constantly re-balancing, just continually, almost daily, re-balancing:

"Okay, what do I have to cancel?" or "Who do I have to be late for?" Like today, for our interview. I can't quite keep it all beautifully together, but at the same time, I don't quite have the personality for someone who has an assistant who organizes their life. I'm a little bit too...what can I say, I have some administrative skills, so I don't mind administrating my own life, in my hodge-podge way.

FOX: Okay, well, that's good. Do you have any questions, Tim?

GREEN: Well, you mentioned yesterday that you took, I think, a three-year break from writing altogether, and you told an interesting story about how you got back into it, but I'm wondering, what was the impetus for that?

PEACOCK: The impetus for the break? I was 21, and the impetus for the break was this: I went to a state university, Binghamton University in upstate New York, and I was the person who was responsible, the student escort, for various poets who were visiting the campus, invited by my teacher, Milton Kessler. So I met Anne Sexton and then she committed suicide; and then I met John Berryman and then he committed suicide; and then I met Robert Lowell and then he was institutionalized. Then I met John Logan, who's a poet whose name you wouldn't recognize, but he was a severe alcoholic.

I had to drive him to an airport on a Sunday morning, and he insisted that we stop at every closed bar on the way. He'd bang on the door of each bar, saying, "I think there might be somebody in there." I was horrified. If art drove you to suicide and alcohol, how could I want to be a poet? Because my father was an alcoholic, because my sister was heavily into drugs, I just wanted to have a normal life. I wanted something calm, something so-called normal—of course, I realized later on that there isn't any such thing [Fox and Green laugh] but I had a dream of this—I mean, I grew up watching *Leave it to Beaver* [all laugh] and I thought this might exist!

So I said to myself, I'm out of here, I'm just not doing this. And I got married to my first husband, I got a job writing advertising, I was constructing a normal life. Except my problem was that I got sick constantly. I got every little horrible cold and bug and virus and flu and everything. I just went around—I mean, I think I blew my nose for three solid years. When I canceled yet something else one weekend because I was sick, my then-husband, who was a very sweet man, said, "You know, Molly, I'm gonna go, I can't stay home another weekend." Who could blame him? I said, "Fine."

I stayed home and I was alone and...I really require a lot of solitude in life, and I had basically spent three years without any. I mean the decision to be normal was also the decision not to have a writing sanctuary and a place to be alone. So the first thing I did was, I wrote a poem, and the second thing I did was, I stopped sneezing. I didn't have to be too self-aware to put these two things together and to decide that I just had to write again, I had to do it, and I had to find a way to do it not modeling myself on people who were so self-destructive or—not that Robert Lowell was self-destructive, he was ill, well, they were *all* ill—but I determined to model my life in more positive, consciously chosen ways. And that took a lot, you know, it's hard to find those models. [phone rings]

FOX: That must be your car.

PEACOCK: It is, it is. Thank you so much for these questions, they're great questions, both of you.

FOX: This was excellent, excellent. Sometimes—it's very interesting, sometimes a poet is not transparent, and just kind of very hidden, and it doesn't work too well—

PEACOCK: No, I'm not! [laughs]

CONTRIBUTOR NOTES

CONTRIBUTOR NOTES

CRISTIN O'KEEFE APTOWICZ: "I find that if I write honestly about an experience which was really horrible and uncomfortable, it will have the pleasant aftermath of coming out as pretty funny. I love poetry's ability to show me that my worst experiences are usually much more surreally absurd and humorous than I had ever realized when I was living them." <www.aptowicz.com>

TONY BARNSTONE: "I was inspired to write this poem while grading papers, because my students read little and talk much. Their culture is an oral culture, and mine is written, and in the gap between those two, human slips in." <www.barnstone.com>

MICHAEL BAZZETT: "When I feel that someone's opened up my head, without using any tools, and somehow given me a new set of eyes, that's how I know it's poetry."

FRANCESCA BELL: "I write poetry in an attempt to draw as close as possible to the world around me and to the people in it. For me, poetry should be intimate, bare, wild, and a little ragged. If you can't go for your own jugular, you shouldn't write."

MICHELLE BITTING: "'Mammary' was brewing for some time, but I kept it at bay until I had the hours and space to write it, not wanting to over think or plan what direction it would take. An old best friend from high school's ordeal was heavy on my mind as I traveled the glorious coastal route from Los Angeles to Big Sur. At a workshop lead by Dorianne Laux, Ellen Bass, and Joseph Millar, I put down the words."

TAMMY F. BREWER: "Recently I watched a documentary on John Lennon in which he told a story about his son who drew him a picture and when John asked his son what it was a picture of, he replied, 'Lucy in the sky with diamonds.' John went on to admit that this was how he came up with the idea for the song of the same name. Hearing this, of course, caused me to feel a connection with John Lennon because I, too, often borrow lines from my five-year-old son and use them in my poems. Be careful if you are standing near me at an airport because something you say may end up in a poem."

MARY-LOU BROCKETT-DEVINE: "I was raised in a fishing family—third generation. 'Crabs' came out of a day on the boat as we were casting our lines with whole crabs in an attempt to catch Blackfish. As I watched the crabs spinning in the air at the end of our lines, I announced, 'We're so lucky crabs never learned how to fly.' The crew and my family members smiled and nodded, having adjusted over the years to having a poet in their midst. I often use poetry to connect my two worlds, and try, as an English teacher, to help high school students connect their real, physical worlds to their writing." <mdevine0447@sbcglobal.net>

CHRIS BULLARD: "I wrote this sonnet in Kim Addonizio's workshop at the West Chester University Poetry Conference. Kim wanted us to invent a new poetic form. I was interested in the ghazal with its repetitive use of the same word in different contexts. I found, as I worked on this poem, that I could create a similar effect within the sonnet form. Call it a sonzal. Kim offered some suggestions on my first draft that I incorporated into this version." <kelltic.bullard@verizon.net>

ERIK CAMPBELL: "I read and write poetry to remind myself that I have a soul that needs a periodic tuneup."

WENDY TAYLOR CARLISLE: "This poem was a gift from the circus backyard in my head where a population of freaks and wire walkers, butchers and roustabouts, folks who work animals, a ringmaster and Tom Thumb are careful to keep the elephant's trunk up for the photograph, don't whistle in the dressing room and never look back when marching in a parade. The poem arrived about a year ago, the form later. I write poetry because I can't help it. Given the choice, I'd be a magician, a jockey, or a diamond cutter." <www.wendytaylorcarlisle.com>

PETER COGHILL: "I'm a physicist by profession, and math was my first love, followed by the outdoors. One droughty summer when the parks were closed by fire it was time for second loves and strangely I found myself reading and writing poetry (Louis MacNeice and Carol Ann Duffy, I just loved her). Something that was a complete surprise to me, and my wife. From there it has only grown."

CAROLYN CREEDON: "To me, writing is arranging nests of words, like wood from water for fire: slippery, porous, delicate, changeable, dangerous, breathing, barely balanced objects. I hope to spend my life doing at a lesser scale what Whitman directed for himself: making small wrecks on many fish-shaped islands. Plus, believe me—it beats the hell outta being a stripper." <carocreedon@gmail.com>

T. S. DAVIS: "In 1958, Mrs. Stidham made her third grade class at Patrick Copeland Elementary memorize a now forgotten poem about the beauty of apple blossoms in the Spring. Most of the kids hated the assignment, hated standing in front of the class one by one to mumble through the barely remembered words. But it was different for me. From then to now, for over 50 years, those blossoms have borne fruit." <redhawk27@charter.net>

PAUL DICKEY: "Poems too sometimes get lost. I hardly recall writing the original draft of this poem, but I am sure that I did. When Tim announced a sonnet issue, I found this in my documents folder under another folder called 'Desktop' on my computer. I changed a few words here and there and soon realized my actions were violating the very idea in this poem."

CLAIRE W. DONZELLI: "Before my sister, Grace, goes off to college, my Dad wanted to make sure she could boil water. It turns out she couldn't, so my little brother had to help her. The warmth and laughter of my family inspired me to write haiku. The smiles they have given me will never leave my heart. I also would have never written any haiku if not for exploring new things, just like Grace."

CAITLIN DOYLE: "When I pass the playground on my way to work, I hear children singing jump-rope songs and chanting *ring around the rosy, pocket full of posy*. When any member of my family drops an Alka-Seltzer into a glass of water, he or she can't help bursting into song, just for the joy of saying the words: *Plop, plop, fizz, fizz, oh what a relief it is!* These are the reasons I love poetry. Its roots lie in our basic human need for sonic pleasure, for repetition and variation, for sounds that stick in the ear. I write because I hope to lodge a few memorable lines in the reader's mind." <doylecai@gmail.com>

CHRISTINE DRESCH: "After harvesting a catch, whalers would often pass the hours until the next hunt doing scrimshaw on the discarded skeleton, carving elaborate patterns with their jackknives, and bringing lines into relief with soot or tobacco juice. I try to approach poetry with much the same goal—attempting to make something beautiful out of splintered bone and broken teeth." <c_dresch@hotmail.com>

JEHANNE DUBROW: "'The Cold War, A Romance' comes out of my current obsession: to write about the awful discomfort and ugly beauty of adolescence. Since I spent most of puberty living in the Eastern Bloc, I've been using the language, rhetoric, and imagery of Communism to speak about the tyranny of the teenage body." <www.jehannedubrow.com>

LAURA EVE ENGEL: "Sometimes I think the formal exists to be paired with the inappropriate. Or maybe I just want to be able to justify going commando in a suit. I ponder these things and more as I pursue my MFA at the University of Houston."

JOSEPH FASANO's recent work can be found online or in print from *The Boston Review, The Southern Review, The Yale Review, The Times Literary Supplement, Western Humanities Review*, and *decomP*. He teaches at Manhattanville College. <joseph.fasano@gmail.com>

ALAN FOX: "At some point time runs out for each of us. As Tim Lever, writer of humorous songs, said at one of his concerts, 'When Mozart was my age he was dead for two years.' Sometimes I wonder if I'm dead yet."

MATTHEW GAVIN FRANK ran a tiny breakfast joint in Juneau, Alaska; worked the Barolo wine harvest in Italy's Piedmont; sautéed hog snapper hung-over in Key West; designed multiple degustation menus for Julia Roberts' private parties in Taos, New Mexico; served as a sommelier in Chicago; and authored *Barolo* (The University of Nebraska Press), *Sagittarius Agitprop* (Black Lawrence Press), and the chapbooks *Four Hours to Mpumalanga* (Pudding House) and *Aardvark* (West Town Press). Tonight, in the kitchen, he will combine blesbok venison with chocolate, jalapeño, espresso, and blood orange.

GLENN J. FREEMAN: "I grew up being taught that a poem was some kind of a puzzle, a riddle that a teacher had an answer to and could determine whether I was 'right' or not. I grew up, then, not really liking poetry. But then at a particularly confusing point in my life, a friend gave me Theodore Roethke's *The Lost Son*. Reading Roethke, I realized that here was a man as confused about things as I was; not some theoretical puzzle, but an individual speaking out of his pain, grief, and confusion. Here was a man taking pain and singing as best he could. From then on, I could hear the real voices in poetry and I began to listen."

CAROL FRITH: "For me, writing poetry is a form of translation—the translating of daily experience into a more formal medium. Organizing images and events in this way enables me to share my experiences more effectively. I value the opportunity to share the work of other poets, as well. My husband and I co-edit the poetry journal *Ekphrasis*, which adds a richness and dimensionality to our own work." <carol4mail@aol.com>

ED GALING: "I was 92 in June, and since my memory is still good I like to write about the 'old days.' Seems like they were the best. With the bad economy now, maybe there will soon be another 'marathon' dance!"

DOUGLAS GOETSCH: "This is my second year as poet in residence at the University of Central Oklahoma. The apartment they gave me looks out on the parking lot described in "Writer in Residence," complete with dumpster and stadium across the way. During my first fall here I was struck by the lack of seasonal change compared to my native New York. Instead, I had the rhythms of the vast parking lot, quietly filling up and emptying out throughout the day. I was also doing a lot of sitting meditation, and often found myself feeling lost—though not in a haunted way. Perhaps this was because I'd never lived or imagined living in Oklahoma, and so had no history here. I felt strangely enchanted, the way a baby might feel waking from a nap, pior to any thinking." <doug@janestreet.org>

PETER HARRIS: "I happen to be a Zen priest, but I hope that is pretty much invisible in my poetry. I do, however, try to keep in mind the aphorism, 'Not one, not two,' as a reminder both of the interpenetration of all things and of their irreducible complexity."

LILAH HEGNAUER: "In this poem there's a house I used to live in, a child I used to care for, and a relationship I used to be in. But I'm not really in the poem. What I like about poetry: the way words and phrases, in repetition, grow new meanings and become larger than their origins. I like making strange bedfellows out of phrases we normally use in different contexts."

DAVID HERNANDEZ enjoys talking about himself in the third person, but even more so in the second. You wrote "Remember It Wrong" in July of 2007. You don't remember much from that experience other than typing "babyish" for the first time in your life. You wonder why "babyish" isn't used more often in poetry and why "honeysuckle" stays in fashion despite wearing the same pair of bellbottoms year after year. You remember Toughskins. Their durability. Your grandmother removing grass-stains with a scrub brush. <www.davidahernandez.com>

MICHAEL HETTICH: "'The Wild Animal' comes out of a project I worked on during the summer of 2008, in which I made myself write at least one 'poem' every day and I didn't allow myself to look back or revise until I had reached 200. The hope was to discover a way to go beyond my long-practiced techniques of revision, to get beyond certain habits of mind that felt limiting. I've saved approximately 60 of these pieces, of which 'The Wild Animal' is one." <www.michaelhettich.com>

BOB HICOK is the author of five books of poetry, most recently *This Clumsy Living* (University of Pittsburgh Press, 2007). His other books include *Insomnia Diary* (2004), *Animal Soul* (2001), which was a finalist for the National Book Critics Circle Award, *Plus Shipping* (1998), and *The Legend of Light* (1995).

ERNEST HILBERT: "Among the many childhood memories that strike me from time to time is one of a small, inquisitive boy scaling a tall bookcase as if it were a ladder or a canyon wall, to reach something, though the object of his adventure may never be known or fully understood. I was the boy, of course, and my mother would routinely lift me off before I fell and hurt myself or brought millions of words down in a fatal avalanche. My father, the first in his family to attend college (on the GI Bill), was an avid reader of everything from espionage novels to Pepys' diaries and *The Waste Land*. As a result, I came of age in a modest home with an incredible wealth of books, quite literally thousands of them. As I grow older, more and more volumes gather about me as well, like barnacles on the hide of an aging Gray Whale. I feel an intense animal affection for the books I've read, but I also experience their incredible weight as if it were on my very back. How many things do we actually hold in our hands, feel in so many ways for so long before relinquishing? I use books to help me remember my life, to give that life fuller sense and broader contour. In a way, I still climb that bookshelf, reaching for whatever is to be found on a higher shelf. How can anyone stand to let books go? I can't, and so we have my humble poem on the subject." <www.everseradio.com>

COLETTE INEZ, the author of nine books of poetry, has been widely published, is represented in more than 70 anthologies, and has read her work in colleges and universities, nationwide. Currently an associate professor with Columbia University's Undergraduate Writing Program, she also taught at Ohio, Cornell, Bucknell, Colgate, The New School and Denison Universities, and at the Hunter and Kalamazoo Colleges.

John Philip Johnson: "One afternoon, a long time ago, before you were born, I was reading Byron. I couldn't believe it when, in *Don Juan*, I found him rhyme *gunnery* with *nunnery*. I thought, good grief, anybody can do this. I wrote reams of poetry, lost most of it, and published some. Recently I woke up in middle age, with the children (cinque bambini!) finally able to dress and feed themselves. So, I've been scribbling again, a lot, and editing this time, like a born English major." <www.johnphilipjohnson.com>

Luke Johnson: "Recently, I spent the summer living in a tent in the woods of West Virginia. Nights, I read poetry by headlamp: James Galvin, Elizabeth Bishop, Fred Chappell. Rain storms drummed tarps strung above me, and the poems joined those rhythms, those gales. I'd like to believe they're equally necessary, poetry and rain, with the same capacity to ease and to overwhelm." <proofofblog.blogspot.com>

Mollycat Jones (Christine Potter): "Once I believed that poetry was something to distract my human companion, so I could knock the pens off her desk and swish my tail under her nose. That was before I discovered metrics and rhyme. Christine mostly writes that ridiculous vers libre, for Big Ones as silly as herself. I write for felines everywhere! And I write in form because the anarchic spirit of all cats is an explosive force that needs something powerful to contain it." <Chrispygal@gmail.com>

Stephen Kessler: "When I started writing poems in earnest, as a teenager, I had no use for free verse, but the formal structures and rhythms of English poetry—especially that of Wordsworth, Shelley and Keats—provided the models for my own earliest efforts. In time I became more 'contemporary' in my approach to form, opening up to more unpredictable lyric structures, but my ear had been trained to hear rhythm and rhyme in a way that continues to serve me more than 40 years later. These sonnets were written during what could be called a cool-off lap after translating about 70 sonnets by Borges for his complete sonnets, to be published in 2010 by Penguin. While they are not formal sonnets in the strictest sense, I think they are close enough to give an illusion of sonnetude."

Jeff Knight: "When I was little, I broke open my Etch-a-Sketch to see what was inside. (Curious? It was a fine powder, along with tiny plastic beads.) Still today, looking at the surfaces of things, I feel that urge to crack things open, only now I'm likely to use words instead of a hammer. This can happen with anything from song lyrics to knock-knock jokes, but the way it happens best is with poems."

Lynne Knight: "My mother sang to my sister and me when we were babies, poems she'd memorized (Lewis Carroll and others), poems she made up as she went along. I'm sure my desire to write started with her singing, but she was influential in other ways. When I was wild and rebellious in my 20s, my mother observed that maybe if I stopped living what I thought was a writer's life and actually sat down and wrote, I'd get somewhere. This stung, but slowly, I heeded her counsel; more slowly, I got somewhere. So it seems fitting for my mother to be such an essential part of the poem that won this award. Most deeply, the honor is hers."

MICHAEL KRIESEL: "One drunk and stormy night in 1999 I wrote my first Threesome, spontaneously—three short, skinny poems varying slightly and laid side-by-side. It appeared in *5AM*. That was it, until a few years ago, when a friend suggested I write more of them. Since then I've done variations. Some can be read omni-directionally, like a 3-D haiku, giving the reader different meanings, depending on their starting point."

RACHEL INEZ LANE: "Last year I moved from Koreatown, Los Angeles, to the middle of nowhere in Tallahassee, FL, to pursue an MFA in creative writing at Florida State University. Recently my poetry has appeared in *Los Angeles Review*, and *Boxcar Poetry Press*, and pop culture pieces in the *Orlando Sentinel* and the *Chicago Tribune*."

KEN LETKO: "I was walking on some bluffs overlooking the Pacific Ocean when I noticed a large black dog on the horizon. The off-leash animal was coming toward me on the same trail. When we met, I realized the friendly, smiling creature was nearly pure white because he was no longer walking in his own shadow! I had witnessed 'the power of light.' I just had to write about that." <ken-letko@redwoods.edu>

GREGORY LOSELLE: "Some of the information here is documentary—two years after his death, the children of my grandfather's second wife returned to us the keys to the house their mother had continued to occupy. It had been looted, stripped even of ceiling fixtures (though, tellingly, my grandfather's books were undisturbed, and while salable compact discs had been taken, the vinyl records from which I'd first learned music with him, during wonderful long evenings in the den, were left behind). A drawerful of half-burnt candles had been dumped onto the living room carpet. But some of the information here is mythic or poetic: the sort of scene we imagine in a simple human preference to remember things as they weren't. His clothing, for instance—for as much as it forms the subject of this sequence—had been disposed of by the time I reached his closet, though a box of family papers and his shoeshine kit were indeed there, as were his shoe trees. The saints' relics were, more properly, in his dresser drawer, though I've relocated them for my own purposes; and to my chagrin I found a stack of my manuscripts, from adolescence through my first fully realized works, on a shelf behind where his clothes had hung."

M: "I was widowed at a very young age. My therapist suggested I attend a grief support group to share with others in similar circumstances. When I walked into the room, I was struck by the realization that everyone was at least 25 years older. And while we shared grief in common, the concerns of these older widows were very different from mine. On many levels, we just couldn't connect. I also read stories online of other young widows who experienced similar feelings of alienation in grief support groups filled with older women. I wanted to write about this disparity, but didn't know how to approach it. Then about a year ago, I attended a reading by Lucille Clifton. She told an unrelated story about driving through a forest with a friend, and their joy upon catching a glimpse of a rare albino deer. The more I thought about that misfit deer, the more I realized Ms. Clifton had unknowingly offered me a perfect metaphor for my experience. I became the albino deer, and I hope that my poem will speak to other young widows who find themselves lost among the elders of the herd." <mjmnv@hotmail.com>

AUSTIN MACRAE discovered sonnetry eight years ago, and since then it has become a full-blown addiction. He attends SWA (Sonnet Writers Anonymous) meetings faithfully each month where he serves as both group leader and engaged participant. His newest chapbook, *Graveways*, is available from Modern Metrics Press at <www.modern-metrics.com>.

MARIE-ELIZABETH MALI: "After reading Neruda's *Poetry* while on vacation, I stood in the INS line at JFK and vowed to dedicate myself fully to poetry. I left my Chinese Medicine practice shortly after and have completed the MFA in poetry program at Sarah Lawrence College. I love how a poem can upend a person's life." <www.floweringlotus.com>

KERRIN MCCADDEN: "I really like water, and birds—especially The Winooski River and swallows. I like to be the one who starts applause. I have recently learned to love olives. I love dailiness, hydrangea, old words and incongruous things, including a poodle. I write poems because they let me have everything I want, and words are better than yarn. Syntax, diction: knit, purl. And because a poem is an impossible thing, unlike a sweater. My evil twin is likely in one of my classes, and so I teach. See some nefarious young people here: <www.hungryrat.com>." <kerrin@mpsvt.org>

PATTI MCCARTY: "I started writing as the result of a midlife crisis, making me wish I'd have had one when I was twenty. But it's probably a good thing that I didn't, because technically that would mean I'd be dead by now, and I have miles to go before I sleep."

LAREN MCCLUNG: "Lately I've been reading the poetry of Anna Akhmatova. She was part of a movement called Acmeism, which formed as a reaction against symbolism. The movement was concerned with poetry that moves through the use of association. Association opens ways between worlds, like the intersection of consciousness and subconsciousness, how one sound or image or thought conjures another entirely unrelated, like montage, like dreaming." <larenm@gmail.com>

MARY MERIAM: "Since I am the voice of a violet crushed by soldiers' boots, I write poems. Since I am the last living passenger out of a subway disaster, I write poems. Since I am a wet quark in a dry universe, I write poems. Since I am a lover's dream of her love, I write poems."

SALLY MOLINI: "I had to write a song in second grade, still remember those four lines, making up the words and then the tune. Expressing imagination through language has always been a big thing for me. I took a letterpress printing class a few years ago and had that same sense of satisfaction and delight working with movable type on a composing stick, each letter and word an inky lingering weight, as if the heft of language were literally in my hands."

JESSICA MOLL: "Since I just wrote a sonnet yesterday, today I'd like to rest. My fingers ache from tapping syllables against the desk. I haven't slept—the loud iambic tick's a clock inside my head. I hate the task I give myself, of cramming my mind's sprawl into the structure of a formal poem. I think the next time that a sonnet calls, I won't answer. I'll pretend I'm not home. But watch, tomorrow I'll be riding down a pitted Oakland street, pedaling hard to get to work on time, and as I spin, I'll feel the meter in my pulse and start to think in rhyme. You've had this kind of lover—as soon as you break up, you're back together."

KENT NEWKIRK: "All the Big Questions, all the little answers—it's not that I don't think about why I write poetry, it's that I haven't arrived at a fit answer. A longtime newspaper editor and athlete, I now cook in restaurants to support my writing and keep my legs strong, believing in exercising the mind and body, putting our heads together under life's collective hood, and helping each other fix more than cars and taxes."

JOHN PAUL O'CONNOR: "*Beans* is a poem I put in the category of what I call time-machine poems. The art shatters the dimension of time to present an alternate reality. This is necessary because our memories are inadequate to represent the past. Just ask anyone from a large family. The same events have different realities according to each memory, each teller. Poetry solves this by making accuracy irrelevant and making something larger than memory. In *Beans*, I flew to my childhood to revive something that affected me deeply and to make something meaningful out of what was irretrievable."

RON OFFEN: "One day, sitting in my high school library writing doggerel to pass the time, my best friend whispered suddenly, 'You know what we should be? Poets!' It was one of those revelations one instantly knows is momentous and right; and I have not stopped writing poems since. A few lines of the poem presented here arrived about 3 a.m., forcing me to get out of bed to set them down." <www.poetsfreelunch.org>

CATHERINE ESPOSITO PRESCOTT: "So much life goes into one poem. This was written after a hurricane in 2005. As my family and I took shelter in the bathroom, we heard trees moaning, pots falling, cars tumbling. Not two years later, I revised the poem after a gun was put to my head during a robbery. After both experiences, I arose amazed to be standing—and grateful that most of my world remained intact, but I saw how quickly all I cared about could be stripped away—and this thought still shakes me." <catherineprescott@mac.com>

JESSICA PIAZZA, born and raised in Brooklyn, NY, now lives in Los Angeles, while pursuing a PhD in Literature and Creative Writing at the University of Southern California. You can check out her most recent work in *Mid-American Review*, *Barrelhouse*, *42 Opus*, *Barefoot Muse*, *Pebble Lake Review* or *Hobart*. Her hobbies include playing with her ridiculous dog Special, Macgyver-style cooking with whatever is in the pantry/fridge, and being your best friend ever. She is powerless against the "The Love Song of J. Alfred Prufrock," grand gestures, cheese, and songs by The Carpenters.

HOWARD PRICE: "My wife of many years passed away and I began to write. And she will always be gone. And I will always be writing. Sometimes you go with a choice not made—one of those imperfections of life."

J. F. QUACKENBUSH: "I am not normally given to this sort of thing, but sometimes a subject calls for ordinary language. As a signifier of honesty, plain language is a little terrifying for me. One must be careful about the appearance of honesty and vulnerability. Such apparitions are rife with opportunities to manipulate and beguile. And also there is a risk of true exhibitionism that is uncomfortable. I tell myself that maybe if I let poems go out into the world where other people can read them, I can gain some distance in the act of letting them go. Maybe that's a self-serving lie I tell myself. Maybe it's a lie I'm telling you to seem more honest. Maybe I believe both."

REBEKAH REMINGTON: "I started writing poetry in high school when I discovered the work of Edna St. Vincent Millay in the school library. I think I renewed her *Collected Poems* almost every week of my entire senior year. Recently I've been reading Frank Bidart, Jennifer Grotz, and Richmond Lattimore's translations of Aeschylus. So I guess my taste has broadened a bit. I wrote 'Happiness Severity Index' on a day when I was feeling slightly whiny."

DAVID ROMTVEDT's "On Broadway" is from a new collection of poems called either *The Age of Risk* or *Cheap Fiction*. You can vote by writing to him. <romtvedt@wyoming.com>

RALPH JAMES SAVARESE: "I grew up in Washington, D.C. with famous Republicans as neighbors. Elliot Richardson lived to the right of us; Frank Carlucci to the left. I went to school and sang in a barbershop quartet with William Safire's son; I played tennis with, and had a crush on, John Paul Stevens' daughter. In college, I discovered that poetry was the perfect antidote to the inane palaver of self-promoting ideologues. It offered a view of the world that was complex, unresolved, intimate, and true. It's saved me ever since."

LAUREN SCHMIDT: "Every summer of my youth was spent in Seaside Heights, NJ, or, if you are from the Garden or Empire State, 'the Jersey Shore.' After spending the day at the beach, my parents would take my brothers and me to the boardwalk which was filled with games, arcades, and rides. When we grew to be too old for these things, my father taught us 'the dollar trick' where one of us would go under the boardwalk with a buck, slip it through the cracks and yank it away as someone reached for it. Some people would laugh at themselves and even become part of the crowd that gathered to watch others fall for the gag. Some people would stomp off all embarrassed or yell through the cracks demanding to know who was behind the treachery. And had it not been for my father who stopped him, one guy would have chased my brother down the beach. I come from a long line of observers, people-watchers, and I believe my summers at the Jersey Shore were the earliest lessons I had in what has become the basis for my poetry." <schmidt613@yahoo.com>

MATHER SCHNEIDER: "Like much of my poetry, this poem is 90% true. One very hot night me and my girlfriend, who is an illegal immigrant from Hermosillo, Mexico, were in bed pushing the blanket onto each other and back again, and it settled in the middle. She called it 'The Border' and I laughed. I knew there was a poem there. Then the image of the wall, dumpster, and connection to the other wall on the border of Mexico and the United States all came together with the idea of walls or borders between people themselves."

PRARTHO SERENO, California Poet in the Schools, has spent the past ten years hanging out with mystic poets, i.e., her students in fifteen schools in Marin County. Anything she gets right in her poems she owes to them, especially the second graders.

LEE SHARKEY: "The immediate trigger for 'Berlioz' was a brief account in Oliver Sacks' *Musicophilia* of Berlioz's turning down the muse. I was struck by the parallels with my own experience of lucid memory—a house fire that devoured among other things seventeen years of my writing, my books, my child's drawings, and my dog—and that earlier, involuntary loss became the emotional driver of the poem. The first line came to me, announcing its rhythm, and I knew from the start that 'Berlioz' would be written in syllabics." <www.leesharkey.net>

PAUL SIEGELL: "What are you gonna do when two good friends tell you this crazy story and you can see the whole thing being played out in a Word doc? You know the scene has more life to it. That it can *do* more. That others would wanna get in on it as well. So whaddaya do? You get your roar to your computer and nail the beast down. Immediately, if not sooner." <paulsiegell.blogspot.com>

CHARLIE SMITH: "I wish I could give you some info about how I wrote the poem, but I can't remember. I was probably walking around, humming, drinking a limeade. The weather now I think about it was cold."

PATRICIA SMITH's fifth book of poetry, *Blood Dazzler* (Coffee House Press), chronicles the human, physical and emotional toll exacted by Hurricane Katrina, and was a 2008 National Book Award Finalist. Her other books include *Teahouse of the Almighty* (Coffee House Press), *Close to Death* (Zoland Books), *Big Towns, Big Talk* (Zoland) and *Life According to Motown* (Tia Chucha).

JOHN L. STANIZZI: "It occurred to me that generations upon generations have been 'practicing' in one way or another for some terrible 'thing.' We have been rehearsing so that we will know just what to do when the unthinkable happens. This is the myth around which my poem swirls." <jnc4251@aol.com>

ALISON TOWNSEND: "This poem arrived for me in almost exactly the way it is described in the piece. I was on my way home from work, in pain from the effects of a long commute on a healing broken back. I was stopped at a light in my small, Midwest town, when I happened to hear a clip on NPR about the only recording of Virginia Woolf's voice that has survived. Woolf's writing has always been important to me, and I was stunned by the sound of her living voice. That set off a stream of associations and I made the leap from Woolf's voice to that of my own mother, who died when I was a young girl and whose voice I have forgotten. When I got home, I listened to the clip again, sat down, and wrote the poem. Knowing more than I did (as our poems always do), the poem made the connections and circled back to Woolf's concept of the 'lamp in the spine' of female intelligence. I felt lucky to have had that moment, where something that felt so difficult in the moment was transformed. All the italicized words are from the recording, except for the phrase, 'the lamp in the spine,' which appears, famously, in her writing."

EMILY KAGAN TRENCHARD loves poetry because it cracks the skull open in much the same way science does. It illuminates and tickles, demands discovery, and insists upon a struggle with contradiction and complexity. Emily is always trying to reach these goals in her own writing and in her role as co-curator of the louderARTS Project Reading Series in New York City. Though poetry is a large part of her creative life, she has a Master's degree in Science Writing from MIT and makes her living in multi-media science communications, helping the public become fascinated by everything from cholesterol to cosmology. <emily@louderarts.com>

ARTHUR VOGELSANG: "I know we are not supposed to depict things as finally horrible, but I did it anyway. There may be consolation in the fact that the two speakers are sleeping, but I don't think so." <arthury123@aol.com>

ELIZABETH KLISE VON ZERNECK: "I used to write fiction, and the first line of this poem was one I had in my head for years as the first sentence of a story. Nothing came of it. When I started to write poetry, I recalled the line—iambic, after all—and the poem followed quickly, almost as if it wrote itself. It knew what it wanted to be more than I did." <eklise@aol.com>

DAVID WAGONER has published eighteen books of poems, most recently *A Map of the Night* (U. of Illinois Press, 2008) and ten novels, one of which, *The Escape Artist*, was made into a movie by Francis Ford Coppola. He won the Lilly Prize in 1991 and has won six yearly prizes from *Poetry* (Chicago). He was a chancellor of the Academy of American Poets for 23 years. He has been nominated for the Pulitzer Prize and twice for the National Book Award. He edited *Poetry Northwest* from 1966 to its end in 2002. He is professor emeritus of English at the University of Washington.

THOM WARD: "The first equation I try to remember: Expectation plus reality equals disillusionment. The next move is then, How to maintain a semblance of sanity in this our human existence? For me, it's the reading and writing of poetry. Then again, that sounds so pretentious I'd like to puke the cornflakes I didn't eat this morning. But I did have a vodka martini, straight up, cold as a glacier, with two olives, wedged into the bottom of the glass, like two dead sailors." <www.custom-words.com/ward.html>

MIKE WHITE: "I'll often begin writing a poem on a subject about which I know little or nothing. This is the 'mucking around' phase, and sometimes (usually) the poem founders quickly. But at other times, a poem about, say, rodeo clowns, will take a sudden and unexpected turn for the personal, and then I know I have the bull by the horns." <mpw3@utah.edu>

DONALD MACE WILLIAMS: "I couldn't remember the name of the effect that has to do with the speeding up of water when its conduit is narrowed (and therefore the slowing down when the conduit is widened), but a niece of my wife's who is a hydraulics engineer helped me with the term. Other possibly pertinent facts are that I live close to Palo Duro Canyon in Texas and am 80 years old." <donaldmacewms@gmail.com>

JEFF WORLEY: "My fellow Kansan Bill Stafford was one of my earliest influences as I began to try to make my way as a poet, and after I met him at the University of Cincinnati in 1984, we corresponded fairly regularly. I think Bill would like this little poem, and I'm happy to have him 'introduce' it in an epigraph." <jworley@uky.edu>

JOHN YOHE: "I wrote this poem in late 2001 or early 2002, and found working within a form helped me say things I wouldn't have normally said. I had been thinking about the 9/11 attacks, wondering how Frank O'Hara would have responded and, in the same way he talked to the sun, I decided to talk to him. The phrase 'the ghost of Frank O'Hara' was in iambic, the rest of the poem sort of flowed out." <yohejohn@yahoo.com>

RATTLE
ORDER FORM
(please print clearly)

NAME _____

ADDRESS _____

CITY_____ STATE_____ ZIP _____

PHONE _____

EMAIL _____

SUBSCRIPTIONS:

[ ] $18 for 1 year (2 issues)
[ ] $30 for 2 years (4 issues)
[ ] $36 for 3 years (6 issues)

Start subscription with issue # _____

BACK-ISSUE CLEARANCE SALE

	Price	Issue #	Conversations with	Tribute to
[ ]	$10.00	31	Toi Derricotte / Terrance Hayes	African Americans
[ ]	~~$10.00~~ $6.00	30	Robert Pinsky / Natasha Trethewey	Cowboy/West Poetry
[ ]	~~$10.00~~ $6.00	29	Marvin Bell / Bob Hicok	Visual Poetry
[ ]	~~$10.00~~ $6.00	28	Tess Gallagher / Arthur Sze	Nurse Poets
[ ]	~~$10.00~~ $6.00	27	Patricia Smith / Marc Kelly Smith	Slam Poetry
[ ]	~~$10.00~~ $6.00	26	Jack Kornfield / Jane Hirshfield	GreatestGeneration
[ ]	~~$10.00~~ $6.00	25	Hayden Carruth / Mark Jarman	The Best of RATTLE
[ ]	~~$8.00~~ $6.00	24	Denise Duhamel / Gregory Orr	Filipino Poets
[ ]	~~$8.00~~ $6.00	23	Alan Shapiro / David St. John	Lawyer Poets
[ ]	~~$8.00~~ $6.00	22	Sam Hamill / Deena Metzgar	Poets Abroad
[ ]	~~$8.00~~ $6.00	21	Li-Young Lee / Naomi Shihab Nye	Vietnamese Poets
[ ]	~~$8.00~~ $6.00	20	Maxine Kumin / Colette Inez	Italian Poets
[ ]	~~$8.00~~ $6.00	19	Robert Creeley / Gerald Stern	20-Minute Poem
[ ]	~~$8.00~~ $6.00	18	Lucille Clifton / Charles Simic	Teachers
[ ]	~~$8.00~~ $6.00	17	Mark Doty / Sharon Olds	Pulitzer Winners
[ ]	~~$8.00~~ $6.00	16	Stephen Dobyns / C.K. Williams	Boomer Girls
[ ]	~~$8.00~~ $6.00	14	Simon Ortiz / Anne Waldman	Native Americans
[ ]	~~$8.00~~ $6.00	12	James Ragan / Luis Rodriguez	Latin/Chicano
[ ]	~~$8.00~~ $6.00	11	Daniel Berrigan	Editors
[ ]	~~$8.00~~ $6.00	10	Philip Levine	Poets in Prison

While supplies last: Buy any five back-issues, and receive a *FREE* one-year subscription!

PLEASE MAKE CHECKS PAYABLE TO RATTLE

Comments:

2010
RATTLE
POETRY PRIZE

1st prize: **$5,000**

plus TEN $100
honorable mentions

Guidelines:

1) Entry fee of $18.00 includes a one year subscription to RATTLE.

2) Open to writers, worldwide; poems must be written in English (no translations).

3) Submissions will be judged in a blind review by the editors of RATTLE: Send no more than four poems per entry; print name, address, phone number, and the titles of the poems onto a cover-sheet. No contact information should appear on the poems. Include a check or money order for $18.00, payable to RATTLE.

4) No previously published works, or works accepted for publication elsewhere. No simultaneous submissions. The previous year's 1st prize winner is disqualified from entry.

5) Manuscripts will not be returned; include a SASE or email address to be notified of the results.

6) Winners will be announced no later than September 15th, 2010, and those poems will be published in the Winter 2010 issue of RATTLE. Additional entries may also be offered publication.

7) Online payment and entries are accepted as well. For more information visit **www.RATTLE.com**

POSTMARK DEADLINE:
August 1st, 2010

Send entries to:
RATTLE
12411 Ventura Blvd
Studio City, CA 91604

RATTLE

Poetry for the 21st Century

Issue #32, Winter 2009

Conversations with
Alice Fulton and Molly Peacock

Editor-in-Chief: Alan Fox
Editor: Timothy Green

"Unpretentious, unpredictable, and ultra-readable, RATTLE is the ultimate in contemporary literature."
—DENISE DUHAMEL

"RATTLE is wide open. Conversations with poets across the spectrum, poetry of every stripe and conviction, reviews and essays—a rich mix for the 21st century."
—MAXINE KUMIN

SINGLE ISSUE: $10.00
SUBSCRIPTIONS: 1-year/2 issues, $18.00;
2-year/4 issues, $30.00; 3-year/6 issues, $36.00

SEND CHECK OR MONEY ORDER TO:

RATTLE

12411 Ventura Blvd
Studio City, CA 91604

Or visit RATTLE online for a poem or review every day:

www.RATTLE.com

A PUBLICATION OF THE FRIEDA C. FOX FAMILY FOUNDATION, INC.

ISBN# 1-931307-17-2